# Healing from Childhood Abuse

D0168929

# Healing from Childhood Abuse

## Understanding the Effects, Taking Control to Recover

John J. Lemoncelli, EdD

*Foreword by Robert S. Shaw, PsyD, ABPP*

 PRAEGER

AN IMPRINT OF ABC-CLIO, LLC
Santa Barbara, California • Denver, Colorado • Oxford, England

Copyright 2012 by John J. Lemoncelli, EdD

All rights reserved. No part of this publication may be reproduced, stored in a retrieval system, or transmitted, in any form or by any means, electronic, mechanical, photocopying, recording, or otherwise, except for the inclusion of brief quotations in a review, without prior permission in writing from the publisher.

**Library of Congress Cataloging-in-Publication Data**

Lemoncelli, John Joseph.
   Healing from childhood abuse : understanding the effects, taking control to recover / John J. Lemoncelli ; foreword by Robert S. Shaw.
     p. cm.
   Includes index.
   ISBN 978-0-313-39788-2 (hardback)—ISBN 978-0-313-39789-9 (ebook)   1. Adult child abuse victims—Rehabilitation.   I. Title.
   RC569.5.C55L449   2012
   616.85'8223903—dc23      2011050347

ISBN: 978-0-313-39788-2
EISBN: 978-0-313-39789-9

16   15   14   13   12     1   2   3   4   5

This book is also available on the World Wide Web as an eBook.
Visit www.abc-clio.com for details.

Praeger
An Imprint of ABC-CLIO, LLC

ABC-CLIO, LLC
130 Cremona Drive, P.O. Box 1911
Santa Barbara, California 93116-1911

This book is printed on acid-free paper ∞

Manufactured in the United States of America

This book discusses treatments (including types of medication and mental health therapies), diagnostic tests for various symptoms and mental health disorders, and organizations. The author has made every effort to present accurate and up-to-date information. However, the information in this book is not intended to recommend or endorse particular treatments or organizations, or substitute for the care or medical advice of a qualified health professional, or used to alter any medical therapy without a medical doctor's advice. Specific situations may require specific therapeutic approaches not included in this book. For those reasons, we recommend that readers follow the advice of qualified health care professionals directly involved in their care. Readers who suspect they may have specific medical problems should consult a physician about any suggestions made in this book.

## DEDICATION

*To the Great Spirit*
*who is the true Healer*

*To my wife, Peggy*
*my best friend and soul mate*

*To all my patients*
*who have taught me so much*

*To you, the reader*
*that you may find consolation, hope, and healing*

# Contents

# Foreword

This book is written directly to the individual who has experienced the pain and suffering that result from abuse/trauma. Dr. Lemoncelli reaches out to the individual from his years of experience working with abuse/trauma in a deeply personal way that is undergirded by solid theory, research, and professional practice. The case examples contained in this book bring to life his proposed theory and treatment protocol designed to assist survivors to gain genuine insight into the effects of abuse/trauma. The case examples clearly demonstrate to the reader that they are not alone in their suffering, thereby reducing the isolation that is so common among the survivors of abuse/trauma.

This book is filled with empowering messages of and from survivors as well as the consistent themes of hope, resilience, and encouragement. However, Dr. Lemoncelli skillfully and compassionately identifies the fears and trepidations that one might experience as they journey to recover.

What especially impressed me about this book is that Dr. Lemoncelli takes on the role of a coach and confidant, constantly working to validate and normalize the feelings and emotions that typically result from abuse/trauma. He uses a significant amount of reframing to assist the individual to see strength where he or she saw weakness and to see resilience where once he or she saw chaos and confusion. He is able to take complex psychological issues and present them in a manner where they are readily understood by the surviving victims. The metaphor of the parasite and the parasite model are well grounded in both biology and psychology. The parasite model allows the individual to make a therapeutic distinction between the self and the abuse/trauma, and to come to believe that the abuse/trauma is only a part of the person, not all of the person. Dr. Lemoncelli outlines 14 stages to assist the individual in his or her recovery and yet encourages the survivor to use these stages only as a guide, rather than a recipe for recovery. He constantly reminds the individual to begin to trust the self because the keys to recovery lie inside of the individual despite what he or she and others have told the individual for years, perhaps a lifetime. As a competent professional, the author tells the reader he is making recommendations, not mandates.

While this book is written directly to the individual who suffered abuse/trauma, it is also indirectly written to the caring ones around the survivor—companions, spouses, friends, and family—to provide them with a solid and dramatic appreciation of the effects of abuse/trauma. Dr. Lemoncelli does this in a manner to assist the caring ones, not to excuse or overlook the self-destructive behaviors of the survivor, but rather to understand the complexity of the effects of abuse/trauma. Equipped with a better understanding of the self-destructive behaviors, the caring ones will be able to directly assist the survivor in the survivor's road to recovery. Lemoncelli constantly reminds the survivor that he or she is not responsible for the abuse/trauma with its resulting pain and suffering, but the survivor is responsible to heal the pain and suffering.

Finally, I believe this book is a great benefit, a *must read* for any clinician working with survivors of abuse/trauma. This book should serve as a text, or at least required reading, for courses designed to teach clinical trainees about the effects of childhood and adolescent abuse/trauma, and how to assist the survivors in their journey of recovering.

*Robert S. Shaw, PsyD, ABPP*
*Director, Counseling/Student Development Center*
*Marywood University, Scranton, PA*
*Board Certified, Clinical Psychology*
*American Board of Professional Psychology*

# Acknowledgments

Throughout the course of my life, my father, Sam "Pop," attempted to teach me many things. One thing he did instill in me is gratitude. One of my favorite quotes from my dad is:

"A man comes into this world with many flaws

And leaves this world with even more flaws

One of those flaws need not be ingratitude."

There have been so many people who supported, guided, and encouraged me that it would be impossible to mention all of them individually. So, to those people who are not mentioned individually, especially my patients who had the courage to allow me to tell their story, know how grateful I am. My heartfelt gratitude goes to each and every one of you.

There are some people I need to recognize in a special way.

My daughter, Mauri, who pushed, prodded, supported, and was so honest.

My mom, Jean; my sister, Cathy; my son, Mark; and his wife, Nicole, who always were there to listen.

My colleagues, Drs. Fedrick, Crawley, Cannon, Muse-Burke, Ahmed, Barna, and Janey.

Beth Graziano, my right arm, who always has my back.

Patti Kurilla, who is always willing to help.

Dr. Samuel Knapp, a kind and brilliant man who is a true inspiration to me.

Carmen Ambrozino, who has blessed us with his friendship.

Dr. Joseph Verga, an admired clinician.

Dr. Robert Shaw, director of Marywood's counseling center and an asset for our students.

Dr. Guido Boriosi, my mentor.

Dr. Anthony Galdieri, who continues to be a colleague and a friend.

Debbie Carvalko, my Praeger editor who has provided invaluable direction.

Toni "TJ" Jones, who knows how much she means to us.

And my wife, Peggy, who has never stopped believing we could do this, my love forever and two days.

# Introduction

Abuse is a horrible, senseless act, or acts. Abuse is a life-altering experience, leaving the innocent victims to carry all the weight of the trauma they have endured. Abuse can be insidious or abrupt. Abuse can be chronic or acute. Abuse destroys the ability of the victims to trust themselves and others. Some victims have carried these burdens their entire lives because they could not share the shame, the guilt, and the tremendous burden of responsibility they carried for what happened to them. "I could not tell anyone. I already felt dirty and damaged. If I told someone, then he/she would know just how dirty and disgusting I truly am. I had to keep up the facade," said Candice, a then 45-year-old nurse who was physically and emotionally abused by her stepmother for 18 years. This incredible pain resulted in these individuals feeling broken, damaged, and something less than those who have not suffered abuse and/or trauma in their childhood. I have worked with patients for months before they began to trust me with the horrors they had experienced in their childhood. I have seen the pain on their faces as they shared their past with me. After seven months, Jim, a 33-year-old construction worker, said, "I really do not want to tell you about my past, but I know I must, if I am going to survive. I have never trusted anyone, but I think I can trust you. I can only hope you will not think less of me." And then Jim began to tell the story of his sexual abuse by his Little League coach. These patients and so many others like them taught me how important it is that someone appreciate and validate how twisted and torn they've felt for years. It was critical to their healing that someone was able to validate their pain. I know how vital this validation is for you. I have witnessed the magical resilience people have when they choose to begin to shed the irrational guilt, shame, and responsibility, to become a survivor and not remain a victim. Later in this book, you will meet Danielle. She will be just one of the many examples of the magical resilience when one commits to becoming a survivor.

You may be struggling not to be a victim and not to be one of them. This text is written in the hope that it will assist you in your struggle to recover from the horrible trauma of abuse. It is written directly to you, the victim, to provide you with as much understanding as possible, to aid you in your healing. (In order to provide clarity, when I use the pronoun *you* I am speaking directly to you, the victim, and when I use the pronoun *we* I am referring to you and me.) It is written with the faith and hope in you that you can and will become a true survivor. Let me begin by firmly stating that, for the most part, what happened to you will never truly make sense. The focus is not to understand the abuse or the abuser but rather to understand your responses to the abuse and how these responses continue to impact your thoughts, feelings, and behaviors today. Equipped with this understanding, you can begin the journey of recovering from your abuse. The goal of this text is to provide you with a true sense of hope and convince you that you are not confined to live in the past. You can begin living in the present with a renewed sense of who you are and that you are not just a victim—you are a survivor.

First, and foremost, the intent of this book is to provide you with hope that you too can begin your recovery. The stories of my patients in this book are all true. In compliance with the American Psychological Association's Code of Ethics, I obtained releases of information for full disclosure. Of course, steps have been taken to protect their identity, but all these patients wanted their stories to be told. They felt that if someone could be helped by their experiences, it would provide them a greater sense of meaning. It is hoped that their stories give you inspiration and that my patients derive a greater sense of purpose and meaning for their suffering. These patients also believe that a book of this nature is important for counselors, psychologists, social service workers, and students in these related fields to obtain a greater understanding of the effects of abuse/trauma on victims and the process to aid the victims in recovery.

This text is one man's heartfelt attempt to help you sort out what has happened to you because of the trauma you experienced. More important, I want to share with you the concepts that have helped so many of my patients curtail many of their self-abusing behaviors and become true survivors. They have learned to either eliminate or significantly decrease the shame, guilt, and responsibility for what happened to them. The emphasis of this text, then, will be directed at understanding what has happened, at appreciating how you attempted to adapt to an insane world, and at learning how to ease some, if not all, of the devastating pain your abuse/trauma has caused. I have been asked the burning question that I am sure is on your mind. The burning question is, "Why?" or "Why me?" Regrettably, that is a question I cannot answer because I simply do not know. What I do know is that you are not responsible. You did not deserve the abuse. You did nothing to engender it. You are not damaged. You are not a horrible person. You are not alone in your suffering. Perhaps life is more a roll of the dice than we want to imagine. Perhaps someday, if there is a Higher Power or a Creator, the Higher Power or Creator will explain the haunting "Why?" or "Why me?" answer. But for now, suffice to say, a person or persons in your life path chose to violate your personhood. This violation resulted in your loss of a sense of safety and security, which are so critical to healthy growth and development.

I will help you appreciate how this violation of your personhood, or violation of boundaries, created significant challenges in your growth and development. This will be detailed in chapter 4 on the impact of abuse/trauma on child and adolescent development. But before I go any further, I need to address some basic theoretical aspects of stress, abuse, and trauma. I will keep it short and simple, but the background is essential for understanding what happened and is a necessary component to your healing. So, bear with me for a few moments.

## BACKGROUND

Childhood abuse is not a new "sin." We need only look at history to see all forms of childhood abuse. However, what is new is the basic understanding of how devastating abuse is to the individual. This can and often does overshadow a person's whole life. Before we get into some of the theory, I want to share with you one of my career-changing stories. I went to high school with Tammy. Tammy, in our freshman and sophomore years, was a happy, kind, and quiet young girl who was liked by most of the class. At the end of our sophomore year, Tammy's father left Tammy and her mother. No one knew the details, but Tammy began to change. This genuinely happy person became a loner. In her junior year, we started to notice bruises on Tammy's face, arms, and legs. When asked what happened, Tammy would just become very angry. The bruising intensified and so did Tammy's anger. After high school, I lost touch with

Tammy. When we next met, we were both in our late 30s, but Tammy looked like she was in her 60s. She knew I had become a psychologist and asked me if we could talk. Tammy confided to me that she had spent most of her adult life in psychiatric hospitals. Her mother was an alcoholic who blamed Tammy for her father's leaving. The bruising, as I am sure you surmised, was the result of the repeated beatings Tammy's mother inflicted on her. Tammy told me that her mother would taunt her about her not being good enough as a daughter, and that was the reason her father left them. So not only did Tammy feel guilty for her father's leaving, she also felt completely inadequate as a person. Tammy said she told the staff at the hospitals her secret and their advice to her was to get over it. I remember walking away from our encounter with many conflicted feelings. I could only hope that Tammy would reenter therapy with someone who would validate her pain. How could anyone tell her to just get over it? Why didn't someone see what was happening to this previously happy young woman? How could a mother do this to her own daughter? In order to begin to truly comprehend the impact that abuse/trauma has on an individual, we need to examine the concept of stress. Moreover, we need to appreciate the impact stress has on the physiological, psychological, and spiritual aspects of an individual.

There has been considerable research on stress, especially in recent years. However, much of what has been written appears to be confusing and at times contradictory. The word *stress* is often associated with something harmful, an upsetting influence, or a disturbance to our psychological equilibrium. Yet, stress also occurs when we are challenged, excited, or joyful. The exhilaration of victory and/or the intensity of passion produce many of the same physiological stress responses as defeat, danger, or frustration (Monat & Lazarus, 1977). It would appear that stress is constant and that it occurs even as we sleep. An integral aspect of life is maintaining a manageable amount of stress.

Hans Selye was a pioneer in stress research whose concepts have served as a focal point for the majority of stress research. From the results of his experiments, Selye (1974) defined stress as "the nonspecific response of the body to any demand." The stressor can be positive or negative, and the stressor is often referred to as a threat because it will disturb our sense of physiological and psychological equilibrium. No matter what the specific stimulus (or stressor) is, a common and nonspecific stress response occurs. For example, suppose you received a certified letter telling you someone left you $100,000 in his will. This is obviously a positive stressor. What would be some of your physical sensations? You might experience some or all of the following: a dry mouth, some perspiration, a rise in blood pressure, weakness in the legs, perhaps dizziness, and so forth. Do you see how the stressor disturbed your physiological equilibrium? And what might you be experiencing psychologically? You might be experiencing joy, relief that you can pay some of your bills, excitement because you can go on that vacation, and so forth. Do you understand how your psychological equilibrium has been upset? Let us now examine what might be perceived as a negative stressor. The certified letter you received this time informs you that someone is suing you for $100,000. What might you feel physically? The body response is probably nearly the same as it was to the positive stressor, with some varying degree of intensity. The psychological response is very different because of our negative perception of this stressor.

Selye (1974) termed the nonspecific response to stress as the "general adaptation syndrome" and further determined that it occurs in three stages: alarm, resistance, and exhaustion. The progression of these stages appears to be determined by the sensitivity to the stressor and the person's ability to adapt. In the alarm stage, the body begins to show certain chemical and organic changes. This is what Walter Cannon termed as the "fight or flight" response (Selye, 1974). If the stress is not eliminated by the excessive sympathetic activity during the alarm stage, the state of resistance or adaptation occurs in the body. The resistance stage is characterized by a mobilization of resources, a rise in adaptation energy, and normalization of the body's chemical and organic functions. During this stage, the individual demonstrates the capacity for attaining a dynamic equilibrium with respect to the interaction with the stress. However, the adaptation energy is limited, and if the body is exposed to a stressor for too long or is chronically exposed to noxious agents, the body enters the stage of exhaustion. This stage results from the depletion of the individual's adaptation energy and signals the return of the general alarm reactions (Selye, 1974). Selye believed that with severe or prolonged stress, irreversible organic changes can occur and an individual could become extremely ill. Selye believed that in many cases the difficulties are not directly caused by the stressor itself, but by our adaptive or maladaptive mechanisms.

When examining stress, one must also take into account that stress is a personalized perceptual event. Now you might be wondering what exactly that means. Take, for instance, a young man who has experienced traumatic physical and emotional abuse by his father. The young man is filled with anger toward his father. If his father were to die, the young man might experience a sense of relief. Typically, in healthy situations, when a father dies, one experiences grief, sadness, and even depression. These negative feelings create the overall experience of distress. However, in this situation, because the young man is actually relieved that his father can no longer abuse him, it becomes a positive experience. But, because feelings are transient, after a period of time, he might begin to feel guilt because he was not saddened by the death of his father. So now he begins to feel distress, not because of the death of his father, but because he did not feel that typical sadness. This demonstrates that the perception of stress is a very individualized concept. The stressor or threat may have very different meanings based on the individual's perception. Perception will be altered by a person's history and the meaning the individual places on the stressor or threat.

When one thinks of the stressors we face in everyday life, one typically views the stressor or the threat as causing the resulting feelings we have about the stress. In reality, it is not the stressor itself but our perception of the stressor that produces the feelings we have toward it. In the preceding paragraph, I used the notions of positive and negative feelings. I need to make it clear that there are no bad feelings. You may have learned that anger is a bad feeling, and when you experienced it, you were a bad person. This is totally untrue. It is not the emotion that is bad but rather how we behave based on our emotion that is then labeled good or bad. Certainly, when we experience anger, sadness, grief, and guilt, the resulting overall feelings are negative. Conversely, when we experience love, joy, excitement, and happiness, the overall feelings are positive. So emotions and/or feelings are categorized as either positive or negative. I want to reiterate again, there are no bad emotions or feelings. Keep in mind that a stressor is determined to be positive or negative based on our perception of the event. Our perception of an event is based on our history, our state of mind at a given time, and the meaning we place on the event. Here is an example that I use in class to explain how perception and meaning determine our view of a stressor. Three women live in the same town and are all the same approximate age, socioeconomic status, and race. They have very similar backgrounds. All three have been married for 17 years, and they all experienced the sudden death of their husbands four months ago. Mary is coping very well and has actually begun dating. Jean remains quite upset but is coping fairly well. Sally is significantly depressed and is finding it very difficult to cope with life. One might suggest that Mary is the healthiest of the three and Sally the unhealthiest. That is not the case at all. Mary had been contemplating divorce for several months. She was saddened by the death of her husband, but also felt some sense of relief in not having to go through what might have been a contentious divorce. Jean's marriage was fair, but she felt for a long time that she had fallen out of love with her husband. Sally believes in her heart that she has lost her soul mate and believes she will never find another like her husband. Do you see how the meaning we place on an event colors our perception of it?

We know that abuse/trauma can occur on physical, emotional, sexual, and even spiritual levels. Some clinicians believe that different forms of abuse/trauma have different impacts on the individual. Therefore, they attempt to treat the effects of the abuse differently. My position, like that of many other psychologists, is that abuse/trauma occurs on a continuum, and because it occurs on a continuum, all abuse/trauma results in a similar clustering of symptoms. We have all heard the phrase "Sticks and stones can break my bones, but names will never hurt me." I don't really believe that's true. Words can be as painful as, if not more painful than, any belt or stick. Likewise, what is often referred to as bad touch is as hurtful as any words or any beatings. The key issue here is that you need never minimize or invalidate your pain. That will serve only to increase your pain. You probably will hear me say this over and over throughout this text because it is such an essential step to the beginning of your healing.

You may have noticed that I have been using the term *abuse/trauma*. It is because I have come to believe that abuse and trauma are very similar in how they impact an individual. Perhaps it would be important to examine the definitions of abuse and trauma. The *APA Dictionary of Psychology* defines abuse as "interactions in which one person behaves in a violent, demeaning or invasive manner towards another person (e.g. child or partner)." The *APA Dictionary of Psychology* defines trauma "as an event(s) in which a person witnesses or experiences a threat to his or her own personal life or physical safety or that of others and experiences fear, terror or helplessness. The event may also cause dissociation, confusion and a loss of a sense of safety. Traumatic events challenge an individual's view of the world as a just, safe and predictable place. Traumas that are caused by human behavior…commonly have more psychological impact than those caused by nature." From these definitions, you can see my belief in the similarity of abuse and trauma. It appears to me that abuse is certainly a traumatic event. I also contend that some other childhood traumatic events such as bullying are abusive. Throughout my experience in treating childhood abuse/trauma, I have found the end result to be very similar in terms of how the experience impacts the individual. Regardless of the type of abuse/trauma, the victims have come to believe that the world is not safe, not just, and not predictable. Because of the loss of the sense of safety, the victim attempts to cope with the terror and the fear the individual feels. These adjustments in childhood are adaptive to their insane world and aid the child in survival, and they become habituated into adulthood when they then become problematic.

Some clinicians view abuse on different levels, with physical abuse held as the least traumatic and sexual abuse held as the most traumatic. This is completely incorrect because all abuse is a violation and all abuse is horribly painful. One of the difficulties that victims encounter is their own attempt to minimize their pain and their suffering. This minimization appears to victims as a way of coping with their pain. The reality is the fact that our negative emotions and feelings are the psyche's way of assisting us to cope with our pain. You may have suppressed all your negative feelings and your pain in order to cope with it. A younger you did not know any other way. It appeared to you that if you dare express it, you would experience only more pain. You said to yourself, "It really was not that bad." The reality is that, yes, it was that bad. Minimizing the pain and thereby suppressing it only serves to make it worse. Attempting to put life events in perspective can be a very positive method of coping. But putting things in perspective can have a positive effect only after the individual has acknowledged the reality of the perceived experience. You must first acknowledge and begin to accept the fact that you were indeed violated, and this violation resulted in significant pain.

Let me give you an example. Jane is a 33-year-old, unmarried, professional woman who first came to me because of an overwhelming depression. In her history, Jane told me that she had a sister who was four years older than she was. Jane stated that her sister was the queen who did everything right, while Jane was the black sheep who did everything wrong. She stated that her whole childhood and adolescence was spent in her attempts to compete with her sister, Alice. Both her mother and father were reported to have constantly badgered her about needing to be more like Alice. When Jane was 17, she and Alice decided to go to a movie during the Thanksgiving holiday. When they came out of the movies, they discovered that it had snowed a few inches, just enough to make the roads slippery. Alice was driving, and on the way home their car was hit head-on by a drunk driver. Jane was injured, and Alice was killed. Jane was discharged from the hospital the day before Alice's funeral. At the funeral home, both her mother and father told her that they wished it was she who was killed and not Alice. Jane also reported that this was said to her time and time again after Alice's death. Jane attempted to minimize her pain by telling herself that her parents were just totally grief stricken. She never acknowledged the pain that she felt from the verbal and emotional abuse she had experienced. She also needed to acknowledge the feelings of rejection that she had felt from early childhood. Only after she acknowledged and validated her pain was she able to begin to cope with it.

When one examines the history of Jane and Tammy, I hope you can begin to understand my position regarding abuse and the need for one never to minimize the pain experienced. Am I suggesting you enmesh yourself in your pain? No, that is not what I am suggesting. I am suggesting that you need to validate your pain in order to cope with it and to begin the process of healing.

# ONE

## A New Approach to Healing

The treatment outlined in this text is based on solid principles incorporating several theories of counseling and psychotherapy, and some basic principles of psychology blended with some principles from the field of biology. Taken individually, these concepts are both readily understood and quite valid. When put together though, the result might raise an eyebrow or two. Yet when I use these concepts with my patients, the concepts appear to make perfect sense to them.

Many years ago, I began to notice that all my patients who had been abused appeared to express the same clusters of feelings and symptoms. There seemed to be almost a universality of the effects of abuse/trauma. Regardless of the type of abuse/trauma, all the patients expressed some feelings of hopelessness and helplessness. They felt consumed by their pain and sick inside. They expressed feelings of worthlessness, guilt, and shame. They all assumed full responsibility for being abused. They were angry and confused. Many of these patients expressed a sense of a thing inside of them that caused them to feel sick inside all the time. Was there a thing inside of them that created these feelings? If there was a thing inside of them, what was this thing? Was it possible that abuse/trauma created a type of illness in its victims? I began to use the notion of an illness with my patients. The patients could readily accept the notion of an illness, and this concept seemed to give them some relief. When my patients would ask me why they felt so horrible, I would simply say, "That is your disease." I would say this not to be dismissive of their feelings, but rather to shift them away from analyzing their pain. When you feel pain, you tend to analyze pain, and this analyzing causes the pain to intensify. Suppose you develop a pain in your left upper chest. You wonder what it could be. It seems to get worse and you go to the emergency room. After running several tests, the doctor tells you that you have a torn muscle, probably from shoveling yesterday's snowfall. Knowing what the pain is brings about some relief. The pain is still there, but the unknown is taken away, and that does bring about some relief. If you continue to ask why you feel this way, the pain will intensify. Remember, the reason you feel this way is because you have a disease.

I know well the great illness debates that occur in the mental health community. These debates have been with us since the 1970s. As a psychologist, I must admit that I, too, was most skeptical regarding the adoption of an illness model to mental health issues. Does an illness model basically say you just need to take these pills, or those pills, to get well? Does an illness model take away the responsibility to actively do things to become well? The answer to these questions is a resounding *no*. Let me give you an example. When my sister Cathy was 23 years old, she was diagnosed with diabetes. There is no genetic history of diabetes in our family. Certainly Cathy did nothing to cause her to become a diabetic. Over the course of years, she developed what is known as brittle diabetes. She has, regardless of diet and exercise, serious difficulties controlling her diabetes, but needs to work at controlling her disease on a daily basis. I present this as an example of the illness model that I use with abuse/ trauma. You, like Cathy, did nothing to cause your illness. While you are not responsible for the onset of the disease, you most definitely are responsible to work at recovering from the disease. The illness model holds the person responsible to work at recovery. No one asked to be abused. No one asked to be violated physically, emotionally, or sexually by someone they trusted. Most unfortunately, you were violated at some level by someone you trusted, someone who was supposed to take care of you and did not.

The disease model that I am proposing holds you responsible to work at your recovering. I use the term "recovering," rather than recover, because recovering connotes a process rather than an event. And based on my experience with my patients, recovering is truly a process. You unfortunately can't just take pills and make it all go away. I truly wish you could. No, you will need to struggle and work hard in order to become a true survivor. The tragedy here is that only *you* can work at recovering from an illness that you have no responsibility for developing. For another example, take a person who has a significant genetic history of lung cancer. Despite the genetic history, the person continues to be a four-pack-a-day smoker and eventually develops lung cancer. I am certain the person didn't ask for lung cancer, but he did place himself in harm's way by his smoking behavior. Considering the illness you need to recover from, you did nothing to put yourself in harm's way. You did absolutely nothing to cause it. You did nothing to precipitate the kind of behavior you experienced at the hands of the abuser. You did not desire abuse. You may have wanted the abuser's attention, but not with a baseball bat or a belt in his hands. You may have wanted the abuser to love you. Not by constantly telling you, "you are a loser and should never have been born." You may have wanted the abuser to touch you, but *not* there and *not* like that. You are not responsible. You are not damaged. You are not a horrible person. You are not less of a person because you suffered abuse/trauma. But something inside you continues to create feelings in you that you are, indeed, responsible. This is your disease.

While the concept of illness gave my patients much relief, it also began to raise new questions. Questions you may be asking yourself right now. So many times I've heard my patients ask the following questions: "But what is this illness or disease inside that seems to make you feel sick all of the time? What is this thing that says to you, 'Go ahead, do it! You are nothing but dirt, and no one gives a damn about you anyhow'?" And then after you do it, this same thing tells you how stupid and disgusting you are for having done it. So many times, I have heard my patients ask the question, "What is this thing that creates these horrible feelings? What seems to seduce me into self-destructive and self-abusive behaviors? How do I get rid of it? Can I get rid of it?" Time and time again I have heard from my patients, "It was like something came over me."

"It was like something baited me into doing something I knew was not good for me."

"Is there something bad inside of me?"

"Am I bad and disgusting?"

For many years, I really wasn't sure how to answer these questions. Certainly I'm aware of the diagnosis of dissociative identity disorder. Years ago, this diagnosis was known as multiple personality disorder. Diagnostically, the concept of this thing inside my patients could be explained by the diagnosis of dissociative identity disorder. However, after performing psychological testing and based on my own clinical observations over time, I could not justify this diagnosis for my patients and, therefore, could not explain the concept of this thing inside of them. However, the more I discussed the illness or disease model with my patients, the more I was amazed by how much sense this made to them. But I needed more answers to all their questions in order to help them recover.

I then began to look to biology to better understand this thing or disease. I wanted to create a metaphor to help my patients and me better understand their disease. It was my hope that if we could better understand the disease that is a result of abuse/trauma, we would be better equipped to assist people in their recovering from this disease. I researched viruses and bacteria and how they can enter the human body and make us ill. Viruses and bacteria really didn't seem to fit what I needed. And then I came upon the literature concerning parasites. Parasites enter a healthy host organism and infiltrate various parts of the host organism. Parasites exist for two reasons: (1) to consume the host and (2) to replicate themselves. I believe the metaphor of the parasite is an excellent fit in understanding what has happened to you. This thing, your disease, your illness, is metaphorically a parasite. Regardless of the type of abuse/trauma you experienced, your abuser fed your ego with contaminants. Sometimes, your abuser told you these ego contaminants were really love. You had no way of knowing that this disguised love was contaminated with the parasite. Bear with me a moment and think about the following statements. "I'm doing this to teach you a lesson." "I did not want to do this: it is your entire fault, you made me do this." "Sure, I tell you you're a stupid jackass all the time. Because you are! I only tell you this so you learn something, but you are so pathetic you never learn anything." "The worst day of my life was when you were born!" "This is the way little boys or little girls love their daddies." I could go on and on, but I hope you're getting the picture. What I am saying is that regardless of the type of abuse/trauma, your abuser infected you with a parasite. Perhaps, the abuser had his or her own parasite. Please do not interpret the last statement as an excuse for the abuser, because there is no excuse for an abuser. It was up to the abuser to work at recovering from his or her parasite, not simply to pass it on to you. This parasite has infiltrated your thoughts and your feelings. If it has its way, it will completely take over your psyche—your soul—and consume you. It will destroy the good person that you are. Please do not let that happen.

And then there are the secrets. The secrets that you dare not tell anyone. Secrets that you bore alone that only served to give the parasite more power. Secrets like, "If anyone asks where you got those bruises, tell them you tripped over the cat. Do you hear me? And they will believe it because you're a jackass and everyone knows it." Secrets like, "If you tell anyone I will kill you." Is it any wonder you feel alone and isolated? Is it any wonder you feel you can't trust anyone? The secrets kept you from seeking any validation for your pain and allowed the parasite to continue to entrench in your ego. As the parasite entrenches into your ego, it begins playing the various parts of your ego against one another. (I will explain this more later.) As the parasite plays these various parts of you against one another, it begins the agony of the abuse–pain–abuse–pain cycle. Long after the external abuse ends, the internal cycle of self-abusive, self-destructive behaviors continues. You could not stop the abuse, but you can and need to stop this internal cycle of continuing abuse. This parasite is cunning and shrewd. If it has its way, it will destroy you psychologically, spiritually, and even physically.

How many victims have destroyed themselves either overtly or covertly? Has the parasite ever consumed the host? Unfortunately, from my vantage point, the answer is yes. Perhaps your own abuser allowed his or her parasite to covertly consume them, allowing the parasite to infect you. I have also experienced patients overtly destroying themselves through completed suicide. I have witnessed patients lose all hope and become consumed by their pain. They continue in self-destructive, self-abasing behaviors and overtly destroy themselves. And what about the people who truly cared about this victim who destroyed himself or herself? Those people feel completely helpless, and hopeless, witnessing their loved one voluntarily take his or her own life. Many times, the family or friends are filled with anger, guilt, or hopelessness. Has the parasite now replicated itself in them?

I realize what you have just read can be quite startling. I am not attempting to frighten you. I am attempting to help you see that you need not give the parasite one more day of your life. I have presented this to reinforce that you are not crazy, you are not damaged, you're not a bad person. You have an illness from which you can begin recovering today. There is more to you than your abuse/trauma. There is more to you than your history; there is your present, and there is your future.

Perhaps we should stop here. If this model that I have presented doesn't really fit for you, that's not a problem. I am sure that some of my fellow psychologists or counselors might have great difficulty with some of the concepts I have presented. If you are currently in therapy and it's working, keep doing what you are doing. If you are not in therapy and this does not fit for you, I would recommend that you find a psychologist or counselor who is less eclectic and more traditional. Perhaps a cognitive behaviorist would be helpful. The important thing is that you get the help you need, and not bear the pain alone. It can be too heavy of a load to bear alone. I believe that no one goes it alone in life. The New Testament tells us that the

Christ fell under the weight of His cross. He needed a Simon, a stranger, to help Him with the heavy burden. We all need a Simon. A therapist can be your Simon. The therapist can help you bear the weight of your cross. Perhaps in your area there is a support group for adult survivors of abuse. I would suggest strongly that you check it out. I know that trust is a major issue for you, but I am asking you to push yourself to develop a trusting relationship with some person or persons. It is critical to your recovery.

Suppose, though, that this does make sense to you and you are already in therapy. I suggest that perhaps you might share this approach with your therapist, particularly if you're feeling bogged down. You and your therapist may like some aspects and use them in therapy. That is great. Use what is helpful and disregard what is not helpful. The important thing is that you work at believing in yourself and your ability to heal, and work at that healing.

# TWO

## The Parasite

Traditional talk or verbal therapy demands excellent communication skills. It is essential that both the therapist and the patient are each able to fully understand what the other is saying. Implicit in this comprehension is the accurate meaning of the words both the therapist and the patient are using. All too often, we use various words that have significant meaning to us but may not have the same meaning to another person. For example, consider a 45-year-old woman had a history of severe emotional neglect from her single mother, and as a result had a great deal of resentment toward her mother. In working with her for about three months, I came to see Linda as a very spiritual person. In one session, I commented to her that I saw her spirituality as a tremendous strength. She promptly retorted, "No, I don't go to church, and I have broken the Commandment of 'Love your mother.'" Linda's definition of spiritual was simply going to church and keeping the Commandments. After explaining what I meant by spiritual, Linda was able to see that she *was* spiritual, and this proved to be a source of ego strength for her. In order to provide clarity between you, the reader, and me regarding the meaning of various words, I will use very specific definitions. This will assist you in capturing the full meaning of the essential terms I will be using. As we continue on in the text, you will notice that there is some redundancy throughout this book. This is not done just to fill up pages. It is purposeful because you will need a certain amount of redundancy to achieve a true understanding of what has happened to you and to help alter your thoughts, feelings, and, eventually, your behavioral patterns. Because therapy is a process and not an event, there is a considerable amount of redundancy as you work through the issues. It has been said that the longest highway known to humans is the highway that stretches from the head to the heart. You know this to be true. Because many things I have told you, or will tell you, you already know. However, getting this knowledge from your head to your heart seems like an endless journey. Taking rational knowledge from your head and embracing it in your heart where you feel it and believe it, is very hard work. Sometimes, it feels as if you are going over and over the same issue. Please be as patient with yourself as you can.

Many years ago, Eric Berne (1961) introduced the theory of transactional analysis in psychotherapy. The author discussed the human need for what he termed "strokes." Now strokes are simply another name for attention and/or recognition. Berne postulated that we humans receive positive attention/strokes and negative attention/strokes. He contended that since we need attention to survive emotionally, we typically would seek positive strokes. But if they were unavailable or impossible to obtain, we would settle for negative attention because without attention we would simply shrivel up and die emotionally. This concept explains how and why a victim would continuously seek out attention from an abuser. Physical abuse is horrible, but it is attention, and to the child, no attention is worse than the abuse. The same holds true for emotional abuse and sexual abuse. We must remember that no child or adolescent says to himself or herself, "Well, tonight I probably will get a verbal thrashing but it is better than not being noticed, or receiving no attention at all." This is purely an unconscious drive. Let me give you a different type of example. Billy is a fifth grader. From all standpoints, he is a pretty good child. But Billy does not really excel in academics or sports. He rarely gets noticed at all. For the last six years in school, Billy has witnessed one of his classmates, Jackie, act out a great deal and receive a great deal of attention. Billy has already internalized that he will not be a star. However, not getting any attention is not working. So Billy begins to act up like Jackie. And now he is getting lots of attention. He is finally being noticed. You may ask, "What does this have to do with abuse/trauma?" I think it explains the cycle. The victim hates the attention he or she is receiving, but at the same time it is better than no attention when no other attention can be obtained. You hated the abuse. You may hate the abuser. But you thought you were bad and disgusting for having these feelings, and that is exactly what the parasite wanted you to believe. In order to cope with your feelings, you attempted to suppress and minimize these feelings. However, this only served to make the feelings stronger. The parasite would never allow you to openly express and validate your feelings.

You may feel you want to hurt the abuser the way you were hurt. It is critically important for you to know that you have a right to that feeling, and simultaneously you have a responsibility to cope with that feeling in an appropriate manner. You do not have the right to inflict bodily harm on the abuser. But you do have the right to feel this level of anger. Once you cease the minimization or denial of your feelings and receive appropriate validation externally and internally, you can begin to cope with these feelings. You may be told by me or your therapist that you do indeed have a right to these feelings; however, it is essential that you internalize this validation and begin to believe for yourself that you do indeed have a right to these feelings.

As I have already stated, validation of your feelings is the first step in truly coping with them. The feelings you have may be quite painful and uncomfortable, and because of this you would obviously rather avoid them. The feelings that you have may, to you, be morally wrong. For example, you may have feelings of hatred toward the mother who abused you. You probably were taught that one should honor one's mother and father. So, to you, this feeling of hatred you have for your mother is morally wrong. I have already discussed the fact that there are no bad feelings. What you must remember is that you have a right to your feelings. Whenever I discuss feelings with both students and/or my patients, I ask them to always remember the two Rs regarding feelings: one's *right* to feel the feelings and one's *responsibility* to cope with the feelings in a socially, morally, and legally appropriate fashion.

Many people attempt to use minimization or denial to assist them in coping with their feelings. If a person is attempting to use this minimization or denial without first appropriately validating the pain, it is like putting the cart before the horse. The feelings just keep going around and around inside you and you go nowhere, and this is how we get stuck in our feelings. I worked with the young man named Jim who was physically and emotionally abused by his father. Jim recounted numerous times how his father would come home in violent rages. Jim's father was an avid sportsman who possessed numerous weapons. He reported that it was not uncommon for his father to chase Jim and his brothers around the house with a loaded weapon. The father had even discharged the gun inside the home on several occasions. When Jim revealed the details of the abuse, I could see the terror on his face. I could hear the total disbelief in his voice. Without identifying and validating his feelings, Jim would immediately minimize the feelings. He would often say to me, "Well, he did not shoot any of us. He only shot at the walls or the ceiling. It could have been a whole lot worse." Yes, Jim was right, it could have been worse. The father could have shot and wounded, or even killed Jim or his brothers. Putting the abuse in this perspective may have helped Jim to initially cope with his feelings. However, the minimization and his attempt to place the abuse in perspective without validation kept Jim stuck in those terrible feelings. He needed to validate his feelings, the terror, the anger, the fear of the unknown, and the fear for his own safety in order to begin coping with them. After several very difficult sessions with Jim, we did not seem to be making any progress. Jim asked me whether I was ready to give up on him. I said to Jim that I was not ready to give up on him, but it appeared to me that he was ready to give up on himself. Jim angrily replied, "What the hell does that mean?" I then reiterated to Jim that he needed to allow himself to feel the feelings that he had from childhood and to allow those feelings to be validated. With this, Jim broke into tears and began sobbing, "Don't you know that it's just too hard?" I then looked Jim directly in his eyes and said to him, "Jim, you're already experiencing the feelings, so as hard as it is let's work on validating them. Jim, you need to share what you are feeling with me." With that, and the sobbing, Jim shared the terror, the horror, and his rage toward his father. I simply kept acknowledging his right to honor and validate his feelings, and how his feelings were normal, and I could certainly appreciate how and why he felt them. He told me he had never shared these feelings with anyone because he feared the other person would find him disgusting. This was Jim's first big step. It was a hard and difficult process, but Jim prevailed, and so can you. I know I have been redundant regarding the notion of validation and its necessity to this healing process. I truly hope you know why I am being redundant, because I know you, like Jim, do not want to go to the depths of your pain. I would not want to go there either, but there is no other way to heal.

Whatever experiences you have had to endure, the key step to freedom from your pain is the validation of this pain. William Glasser has been quoted as saying, "What happened in the past that was painful has a great deal to do with where we are today, but revisiting this painful past can contribute little or nothing to what we need to do now." I completely agree with the first part of Dr. Glasser's statement, and I am not just asking you to revisit the painful past. Rather, I am asking you to validate the painful past so that you can begin to place all of your energies in the present. I use an example with my patients in therapy. Suppose we are soldiers in Afghanistan and our vehicle is hit by an artillery shell. My good buddy who is next to me is dead. His body is almost unrecognizable. I have had my arm blown off. Certainly I know that I am in much better shape than my buddy, but that does not stop my pain, nor does it stop me from wanting to be whole; I want my arm back. Once I validate my pain and come to terms with the fact that I cannot go back and undo what has happened, I am now ready to be in the present and to cope with the present as best as possible.

We need to continue to examine the notion that no matter what level of trauma you endured, all trauma is a violation; it is all a boundary violation to your mind, to your emotions, and to your body. As I have already stated, through this boundary violation you ingested contaminants. This parasite has created a psychological illness in you that causes you to feel horrible. It may take a considerable amount of time before you begin feeling really well again. From time to time, this parasite may rear its ugly head and cause you some distress. But once you are able to recognize it, it does become easier to control. It is a horrible situation. I will tell you over and over again that you are not responsible for the pain you are experiencing. I cannot tell you how to feel, but I can tell you there is no need for guilt or shame. Continuing to hold on to the feelings of guilt and shame will only inhibit you from taking responsibility to begin recovering from this illness. You will need all your physical, emotional, and spiritual energy to perform all the necessary treatment aspects to flush this parasite from your system.

So what we need to do now is to examine the things that were said to you, and done to you, and begin to understand how a child or a younger you may have interpreted those things. Remember in the introduction I spoke about stress and how it is a perceptual event. What I ask you to do is to think about what kinds of experiences you did have and how your younger self might have perceived and interpreted those experiences. The most important point I am attempting to make here, and please listen to the logic, is that if you have ingested contaminants sometimes disguised as love, then there is no way you could have known what you were ingesting was contaminated. You did not ask for contaminated love, you simply asked to be loved as a child needs to be loved. I know that if you were talking about another person, your logic would say he or she is not responsible. But somehow you continue to feel responsible. Recently I worked with a 21-year-old college student. Her name was Greta. Greta witnessed her mother kill her baby sister. Greta was 4 years old at the time, and even at the age of 4, Greta tried desperately to stop her mother from hurting her baby sister. Her mother was tried and sent to prison, but she continues to this day to not take any responsibility for the death of her daughter. Greta, in contrast, holds herself totally responsible for the death of her baby sister. During the course of one of our sessions, I asked Greta to help me appreciate how she could be responsible for what happened. Greta's response to me was completely overwhelming. Greta said, "My mother will not take responsibility, and if I do not take this responsibility, then it is like it did not happen. And it did happen, and I owe that to my sister and to her memory." As long as I have been treating persons who were abused, I never would have conceived that perhaps one of the reasons a victim holds on to the responsibility is his or her attempt to maintain the reality of abuse. What I would say to you, and what I said to Greta, is that you know in the depths of your soul that this did happen. That makes it real. And with that knowledge in your soul you can shed all the responsibilities of the horrible things that happened to you. I ask again that you examine the innocence of the child who unknowingly ingested contaminants. He or she cannot be held responsible for what happened. Unfortunately, the innocent child who was abused is stuck with the responsibility, not for what happened, but rather for working through the effects of what happened and the resulting illness.

Perhaps you say to yourself, "This pain is too overwhelming." Indeed, it may feel completely overwhelming. However, to keep putting it on the shelf and suppressing it has taken and will continue to take a terrible toll over time. Think about this: Suppose you have a pile of garbage in your attic and it is really not bothering anyone. You can smell some odor from time to time and maybe some bleed-through in the ceiling, but it is tolerable. To go up into the attic and to actually sort through all the garbage is terrifying. You might say, "Oh my God, I could never work through all of this." This is the parasite talking. The longer it remains there, the worse the mess. You need to embrace the terror you feel. The terror is healthy, it is a psychological caution light, but it is a yellow light, not a red light. This is where your therapist can be essential. With his or her help, you can take one step at a time and one day at a time. Do not do this alone. The caution light says, "Go slowly, and go meticulously." You cannot do it all at once; that is dangerous. But you can take it on piece by piece, and you need to recognize that you really do have that kind of control.

Now, the parasite will tell you that you do not have any control and will attempt to overwhelm you. Listening to the parasite tell you that you really do not have that control is how it reciprocally keeps itself within you. "I am too big, too monstrous, and too terrible for you to deal with, so I am just going to stay here and you are stuck with me. You will never be rid of me." I know these are the kinds of things that the parasite says to you, and it terrifies you, and you believe these things. My simply saying that you do have this kind of control will not make you believe it today. Do not expect to automatically connect with me and say, "Okay, I do have that kind of control." This is where you will need to work very hard to begin to believe in yourself and not the parasite.

The things I am about to say to you may be quite hurtful. The last thing in the world I want to do is hurt you more than you have been hurt. But I need to be honest with you. Once you began to shed some of the responsibility for the abuse/trauma that you carried for so long, you can begin the next step in your recovery. This next step requires you to be totally honest with yourself and admit that what has happened is very real, and no matter how hard you have tried, you can never change the past, and you need to surrender to that reality. You also need to surrender to the reality that you have an illness, an illness you can begin to take responsibility to heal. You have this thing in you that has directed your life. You do not like what it is doing to you. You do not trust anyone. You do not trust yourself. You do not like yourself. You do not think you are good enough. You feel broken and damaged. Whatever the parasite keeps saying to you, you need to begin to recognize that you are not powerless. Your childhood or adolescence is always going to be a part of you. But that is a key point, a part of you, not all of you. It is a part of your history. It does not need to control the rest of your life. While it is a part of your history, there is more to you than just your history. There is your present, and there is your future.

You may find that this surrendering can take a considerable period of time. It is by far one of the most difficult steps, if not the most difficult step, because this is the new beginning for you. I know from my experiences with my patients that this is the step they have avoided most of their lives. It is a true surrendering to the reality of what has happened to you, and a surrendering to the fact that nothing can change this reality. You cannot wish it away; it is what it is. In Alcoholics Anonymous, many individuals rely heavily on the serenity prayer. You probably know it, but for the sake of clarity, I will repeat it here. "Grant me the serenity to accept the things I cannot change, the courage to change the things I can, the wisdom to know the difference." I believe this can have great meaning for you. I know you do not want to accept what has happened. Surely, your life would be much easier if it had not happened. But, unfortunately, humans are incapable of going back in time and changing the past. You attempted to suppress this reality and that does not work. You attempted to pretend your life was different, and that has not worked. Perhaps for the longest time, you have said to yourself, "I am not a victim, I am not one of them." Believe it or not, your unwillingness to accept the fact that you were a victim of childhood abuse/trauma has had only a paradoxical effect, and it is the very thing that has kept you a victim and prevents you from becoming a survivor. Please know that the longer you fight it, the longer you remain a victim. So I am challenging you to surrender to the past and begin to put forth all your power into your present. Channel all your energies into becoming a true survivor. You may not think this is possible, but I know it is because I have witnessed it in so many people like you. I am not asking you to trust me, rather I am asking you to trust in the goodness of you.

# THREE

## The Workings of the Parasite

I wish I were with you so that I could ask you how you are feeling right now. You might say to me that you really do not know how you are feeling or you might tell me that you are confused, perhaps even frightened. After what you have been reading, I can readily understand your feelings. You have just read that you have an illness, and, through the abuse/trauma that you experienced, a parasite has entered your ego, and this parasite is very powerful. The metaphor of the parasite is being used to assist you in your struggle. For a very long time, you felt that you have been at war with yourself. I am suggesting that you consider that you are at war, but not with yourself, rather you are at war with the parasite. I hope that you are also feeling a sense of relief that someone has been able to explain the conflicts you have experienced. Perhaps you even feel a sense of hope that you can begin recovering. So, do I simply want you to pretend that the parasite is not powerful? Absolutely not. We both know this parasite is powerful, and it is cunning. But you are more powerful and you need to work at believing that right now. You may be asking, "How do I come to believe that I am more powerful against this parasite?"

The question you are asking is an excellent one. It is one that I have been asked by so many other people that surely it needs to be addressed. Regardless of how long you have worked at attempting to cope with this parasite, you are not going to change your feelings and your resulting behaviors overnight. The parasite has frightened you, terrorized you, caused you to victimize yourself and played self-destructive games with you. Think about this. Perhaps you woke up this morning and promised yourself you would not engage in a behavior that a part of you knows is self-destructive. But somehow the parasite bates you into doing the very thing you promised yourself you would not do. And after you engage in that be-havior, the parasite starts the negative self-talk. "How could you do that? What is the matter with you? How could you be so stupid?" It seemed to you for a very long time that you could not win regardless of what you did. Now I am telling you that you can stop this cyclical process and take the power back from the parasite.

We need to examine the cyclical process and understand that it is through the cyclical process, the parasite maintains its power and strength. It will take some time and some significant work, at first, to recognize when the parasite is talking to you and corrupting you. You may be saying, "It does not sound like a thing talking to me; it sounds like me." You are right. It is you at some level. However, it is you, infected by this contaminant that is impacting how you talk to yourself, how you think, how you feel, and how you behave. The parasite has infected various parts of your ego, and by playing one part against the other, it continues to make you feel ill. Remember, the function of the parasite is to destroy the host and replicate itself.

You may be asking yourself, "What does he mean by parts of me?" In order to explain this, we need to go back to some basic psychologi-cal theory. (The summaries of the theoretical concepts included in this book are drawn from N. Murdock's 2009 text, *Theories of Counseling and Psychotherapy*.) We all talk to ourselves inside our head. One aspect that I am sure we have all seen is a cartoon depicting an angel on one shoulder and the devil on the other. While it is highly doubtful we have an angel or a devil on our shoulders, we do know that the ego is composed of many parts and that these parts talk to us in our head. Cognitive psychology has for many years understood that human beings have what is known as in-ternal monologues and dialogues. For example, you may need to confront someone about a particular issue. Do you rehearse in your head what you might say to this person? When you are faced with the particular deci-sion, you find yourself weighing the pros and cons in your head. Most of the time, we are not even aware of the chatter. But it is there. Sometimes it may feel like parts of you are talking to you, one saying, "You know you cannot afford this," and the other part saying, "Oh what the hell, you deserve it." Almost like the angel and the devil in the cartoon. This is an internal dialogue.

A key element to understanding yourself is recognizing that the ego has many parts and these parts need to work together in order to maintain your psychological health. This is very similar to how the physical body has many parts and/or systems that need to work together in order to maintain your physical health. If one or more of the physical parts become infected, the result is pain, which alerts you to the fact that something is wrong and needs your attention. We typically think of pain as something very negative because we feel distressed. However, if the person did not feel chest pain, he or she probably would never go to an emergency room and receive proper care. If the person did not experience the chest pain, this individual might have died of a heart attack. In a very similar fashion, your psychological ego that has been infected and fragmented by the parasite has been attempting to tell you something is wrong and needs your attention. The psychological pain you have been experiencing for so long is the ego's attempt to inform you that it has been contaminated and this contamination has caused fragmentation. You need to take the power back from the parasite and work at assisting the parts of you to work together. I am sure that you are now saying or thinking to yourself, "Okay, how do I get the parts of me to work together?" In a way the answer is simple, but it will require a large amount of hard work on your part. The parasite has infected many parts of you with nothing but lies that you have come to believe are true. The parasite has been telling parts of you that what happened to you is your fault. It has been telling parts of you that you did something to engender the pain of the trauma/abuse. It is holding you accountable and responsible, and this results in the feelings of guilt, shame, self-hatred, and the sense of being damaged. You have been experiencing these feelings for so long that these feelings have become your reality and have been integrated into your identity. No one can tell you how to feel. I wish I could tell you not to feel those feelings, but I cannot. You are the only one who can alter these feelings. Yet, I can tell you that there is no logical or rational reason for these feelings. You did no wrong. You did not engender the abuse/trauma. Yes, you wanted and needed the abuser's love and attention. You wanted them to hold you and caress you, not to beat you. You wanted them to affirm you and praise you, not to belittle, to degrade, and humiliate you. You may have wanted them to touch you, not there, not like that. A person or persons violated your trust. A person or persons violated your boundaries. A person or persons violated your personhood, and because of these violations your ego became fragmented. You are not damaged. You need to listen to the internal monologues and dialogues. You need to refute the lies you have come to believe, and you need to believe in the goodness of who you are, what you are, and what you can become. You need to believe that you are not just a victim; you can become a true survivor. This is how you take the power back from the parasite and begin healing the fragmented ego.

There are other critical elements that need to be incorporated in order to assist the victim of abuse/trauma, and these are the concepts of Alfred Adler. Adler proposed that early in childhood we learn many basic mistakes about ourselves and our world. These basic mistakes are what the parasite holds on to within our ego or mind to keep us ill. The key basic mistake within the domain of abuse/trauma is "You are damaged." Until you rectify this basic mistake at both a feeling and a belief level, the parasite will keep telling you that you are damaged. At some unconscious level, a part or parts of you want to believe you are not damaged. This part or parts perhaps even know you are not damaged, but you continue to feel you are. You need to rely on your healthy parts to educate and, more important, convince the other parts of you that you are not damaged.

Sometimes the internal monologues or dialogues are almost like old erroneous tapes that get played from time to time. My mother, because of her history (and perhaps her parasite), was and is terrified of illness. When I was a young boy, my mother would tell me not to ever get my feet wet, because I would catch a cold. Growing up, I became fearful to get my feet wet from rain or snow because I would become ill. Heaven forbid I should get my feet wet, catch a cold, and, more important, disappoint Mom. I know as an adult that a cold is a virus, and you cannot catch a virus from getting your feet wet. Nonetheless, here I am, an adult male, 10 years older than dirt, who still feels yucky inside when I get my feet wet. While this belief may seem somewhat simple, when we dissect it we begin to see how complicated this is. Part of this basic mistake is the fact that I thought I had control over whether I became ill. Another part of this basic mistake is the fact that I thought I had the power and control to please Mom by staying healthy and that if I did not stay healthy, it was my fault that I disappointed her by becoming ill. The reality is that we humans do not ever have that kind of power or control. However, there remain some lingering effects from a basic mistake that has not been completely rectified.

Theoretically, the Adlerian concept of basic mistakes holds true for all of us. I, like Adler, cannot imagine the child growing into adulthood without some basic mistakes regarding himself or herself and his or her world. Let us go back to biology to appreciate the parallel I am making here. Many true parasites cause mild discomfort to the host. A physical example of the parasite that causes only minor discomfort would be tapeworms. Other parasites such as flatworms can cause significant difficulties for the host. The ongoing struggle with flatworms would require the host to seek a medical intervention. The illness of malaria is the result of a parasite. On the other hand, if malaria is not treated medically, it can be lethal. I hold that the basic mistakes of the Adlerian theory are parallel to biological parasites. If you listen closely to what I have just said, it would appear that I am suggesting that all of us have a type of parasitic illness within our ego. That is exactly what I am suggesting. The parasite of abuse is similar to malaria in that if left untreated, it also can be lethal. The task for all of us in adult life is to transform our big basic mistakes into smaller, less dysfunctional basic mistakes.

Many patients told me that the sickness inside of them almost felt like a war was raging in their heads. Perhaps you feel the same way. There are healthy and infected parts inside of you. The parasite will often play one or more parts against the others. For example, at times you may have been very depressed. Say it is six o'clock in the morning, the alarm goes off, and you have to get ready for work. A part of you that has been infected by the parasite says to you, "Oh God, I cannot face another day; I feel so terrible." Sometimes you even internalize these immobilizing feelings. "I cannot get out of bed; I cannot face today. I do not have the energy to get in the shower." You hit the snooze alarm and turn over, and in another 15 minutes, the alarm goes off again. "Oh, no way, I'm not going to work; I cannot face another day." You get up and call in sick. Somehow you feel relieved, almost feeling better. You promise yourself you will get up soon, take your shower, and maybe even do something fun today. Perhaps you sleep until noon and turn the TV on, but you cannot concentrate, and before you know it is five o'clock. You get up for a glass of water and glance at yourself in the mirror. Then what feels like another part of you says, "Look at you, you are disgusting. Get a glimpse of yourself—you didn't even get out of bed today. What is wrong with you? You did not even get a shower. How could anyone truly love you? Is it any wonder why no one likes you or loves you?" And then there is the commitment: "Well, tomorrow will be better." But tomorrow is not, and the cycle continues. This is a prime example of how the parasite plays one part of you against another, baiting you into wasting your day and then crushing your spirit because you did waste the day. It is very important that you become aware of this cyclical process. Each time it cycles, this cyclical process builds momentum, and momentum is power for the parasite. This is how the parasite is able to keep you feeling helpless and hopeless, because the parasite has built up so much power over time. This is your struggle, and in many respects it is a war. However, it is very important that you recognize that you are not at war with yourself. Rather, all of the parts of you are at war with the parasite.

At this point in time, it is important that you begin to put some of these pieces together. Once you come to terms with the fact that no part of you holds any responsibility for your abuse/trauma, and you begin to recognize that you are at war not with yourself but with the parasite, you no longer need to feel like you must eliminate a part or parts of you that you believe caused the abuse. Many self-help books refer to the concept of healing the inner child. For many victims, this healing the inner child is something that can be important. For you, it may be a necessary aspect of your healing. However, it is very difficult, if not impossible, to do because the parasite has you convinced that the inner child is ultimately responsible for all your pain. I have heard so many patients tell me that they hate their child part. They believe they need to destroy that part. Again, this is where the parasite gets its power. It logically tells you that since the child part caused all your pain, you must eliminate this part in order to be pain free. This is similar to the New Testament notions that "if your eye is an occasion of sin, pluck it out" (Mark 9:47). If it is your hand that is responsible for your pain, simply cut it off. In today's world that would be self-mutilation. This type of self-mutilation would probably get you hospitalized. Is that really what you want to do? Do you really want to eliminate a vital part or parts of your psychological being? I most sincerely hope that your answer to this question is a resounding *no*. Yet, this is exactly what the parasite has been conning you into doing. And the result has been self-defeating, self-debasing, and self-abusive behaviors that have only served to continue to increase your pain. You can place appropriate healthy boundaries on a part or parts of you. You can eliminate unwanted behaviors. You cannot eliminate a vital part of your psychological ego.

I hope by now you have at least begun to surrender to the fact that you were victimized. It is hoped that at least you have begun to feel less of a responsibility for the abuse/trauma. Now, with the knowledge of your illness and how the parasite has been playing the parts of your ego against one another, you can begin to radiate the parasite. I know you want the chatter in your head to just stop. I know you want the pain to cease, and I know you want the self-defeating, self-abusive, and self-destructive behaviors to end. All of these things can and will happen, but it will not happen today or tomorrow. You need to be steadfast in your commitment to healing and you need a great deal of patience with yourself. Remember that the parasite gets its power from you struggling against yourself. Be as gentle with yourself as you would be with the most precious person or thing in your life.

You might be asking yourself, "What does he mean by radiating the parasite?" The counseling I did prior to the development of this model of the parasite was, in my mind, metaphorically likened to chemotherapy. Chemotherapy, as we know it, is able to kill off bad cells but oftentimes kills off healthy cells as well. Being able to identify the parasite and the parasitic mantras is much more exact. This, then, would be analogous to radiation therapy as it attacks cancerous cells and not necessarily healthy cells. However, you must keep in mind that radiation can be a very painful process and never quick enough for you because you are in pain. Unfortunately, nothing is ever quick enough when one is in pain. I know you are in pain and I wish you could stop it right now. But I can tell you and hope that you will hold on to this notion that you can begin to shrink your pain right now. Over the course of many years, I have seen patients attempt to either alter or change their behaviors. When one commits to altering or changing one's behavior, one needs to fully appreciate the process necessary for true behavior change to occur. Most of our behaviors are habituated. Habits are very difficult to alter. If you have been engaging in a behavior that is hurtful, I am sure that you want to simply stop engaging in that behavior. But that is not the way humans function. Let us take, for example, the negative self-talk. Rather than simply being able to stop it completely, you need to start catching yourself in your negative self-talk. It is important that you do catch yourself engaging in this behavior and begin to reduce the amount of negative self-talk. You will not be able to simply stop it. This is where the parasite will play on your feelings of defeat because you continue to do something you do not want to do. Perhaps something happened today that triggered the negative self-talk. Typically, you might have spent hours beating yourself up in your head. However today, you caught yourself in the negative self-talk and you were able to alter your thinking after 30 minutes. The parasite will tell you that you are not making progress. I will tell you and you need to tell yourself this is incredible progress. Certainly, you would have preferred not to have engaged in negative self-talk at all. But you reduced the time you spent in this negative self-talk, and you radiated the parasite by not allowing yourself to feel defeated. A solid pat on the back is definitely in order because this is solid progress.

You have heard me refer to the parasite as powerful, baffling, and cunning, and to allude to the parasite as intelligent. I would also say that this parasite has a mind of its own. This may be difficult to understand. At times, it is still difficult for me. Let us examine what we know about various viruses and bacteria. Specifically, let us consider what we know about the avian (bird) flu. We have been told that currently this virus is contained to certain birds and really poses no threat to humans. However, many scientists predict that in time it will find a way to invade the human organism. For me, it would appear that this virus does have some kind of intelligence or a mind of its own. We know that some bacteria have become resistant to many of the antibiotics that we use to treat the bacteria. How can this happen? How are bacteria able to accomplish this? I would suggest that to say the parasite in you has a mind of its own actually has some biological basis. The notion of the parasite's mind of its own or intelligence is simply a way for you to appreciate what it is doing inside of you. As you struggle with the parasite, it will fight back, baiting you to fail and to lose hope. It will not just quietly leave you. You need to begin to recognize when the parasite is attempting to play you. And remember—it plays hard.

Let me give you an example. I have been working with Danielle for several years. Danielle was physically abused throughout most of her life by her father. She felt emotionally abandoned by her mother because her mother never protected her from her father. Danielle reported that during adolescence she was very shy and withdrawn. She had few friends and found it difficult to trust anyone. During her first year of college, she was befriended by a woman who worked at the college. Danielle told this woman some of her history and confided in her that she felt totally unlovable. The woman promised her that she would help her feel lovable and began to sexually abuse Danielle. The sexual abuse went on for several months. Danielle reported to me that she knew something was wrong, but the woman kept telling her that these sexual encounters would help her. At some point, Danielle confronted her abuser with the fact that she felt the woman had seduced her. The woman immediately turned on her, and told Danielle she was the seducer. Confused and feeling ashamed, guilty, dirty, and totally responsible for what happened to her, Danielle began to drink quite heavily. Obviously, Danielle was attempting to self-medicate pain, but now the alcohol was becoming another problem. Danielle began counseling with me when she was 23 years old. She was able to relinquish some of the responsibility for the physical and emotional abuse, but could not let go of the responsibility for the sexual abuse. After all, she would say, "I was 18 years old and should have known better." Through the parasitic model, I was able to demonstrate to her that she already had a parasite from the physical and emotional abuse, and that this parasite set her up to continue in her victimization. After a long and difficult battle, Danielle surrendered to the fact that she was victimized all her life. She has made tremendous progress in her war with the parasite. A few months ago she came to me and said that she believed she needed to confront the abuser's supervisor. This would be an indirect level of confrontation with her abuser. Danielle did not want to face the abuser personally but rather wanted to confront someone in authority over the abuser. She felt this would help her minimize the parasite's impact on her thoughts, her feelings, and her subsequent behaviors. After some lengthy discussions, Danielle was able to accomplish this confrontation. Fortunately, the person she spoke with was very compassionate, very caring, and very validating. The authority figure apologized on behalf of the abuser. For several weeks after, Danielle felt really good about herself and her situation. And then all hell broke loose. Danielle started having incredible flashbacks of the sexual abuse. She found herself driving past areas where the abuser lived, where the abuse occurred, and where the abuse accelerated. Because the parasite is powerful and cunning, this was to be expected. I believe the parasite, with its mind of its own, demonstrated to Danielle that she was not completely healed.

What helped Danielle was the recognition that she needed to persist at what she had been doing and to continue to utilize the techniques that she had learned in therapy. This resurgence of the parasite actually provided another turning point of her therapy. Danielle began to recognize that she needed to discuss details of her physical abuse by her father and the sexual abuse by this woman. We had talked around the details, but she had never fully shared with anyone, including me, the details of her abuse. As she began providing the details, she could feel herself becoming healthier and healthier. Yet, here was where again the parasite demonstrated how coming and baffling it can be. It was at this point in therapy that Danielle said to me that she needed to directly confront the woman who had sexually abused her. Now we were both aware of the reported pathology of this woman. I said to her in a fair but firm manner, "You may need to do this for you. However, I cannot and will not go there with you. If you feel you really need to do this, I will respect your judgment. But in doing this, you will need to find another therapist because I see this as the parasite baiting you into revictimizing yourself. The abuser will never take responsibility. This person will turn around and blame you, and you will reintegrate the responsibility and take it back onto yourself." Danielle and I have had some difficult sessions but that was by far the most difficult.

Do most therapists believe that you should go back and confront the abuser? Some therapists do encourage this approach, although I view it from the standpoint of "what good will it do?" Will it bring about healing, or will it bring about another level of abuse? You cannot simply prescribe the same treatment to everyone because each person is a unique individual. You may have the ego strength to stand up to the abuser and say, "You lousy rotten person, do you have any clue of how much you hurt me?" Whether the abuser acknowledges that fact or not, you said it, and simply because you said it, you may feel better. However, it may be disastrous for you if the abuser denies any wrongdoing. The parasite will then not only reabsorb the pain, but the full responsibility for the pain as well.

Am I saying that you should never confront the abuser? No. Depending on your situation, you may need to confront the abuser at some point. I do not believe that all victims should confront their abusers, but confronting the abuser is not the place to start. By the way, after several weeks, Danielle acknowledged that she actually felt relieved when I told her I would not support her confronting her abuser. She has been doing well since and has been discharged from my care.

Another mechanism of how the parasite works is the fact that it is very good at baiting you into the "if only game." One example of this can be seen with the patient named Katie. Katie came to me when she was in her late 20s. She was suffering from major depression. She felt hopeless and helpless and she had thoughts of suicide. Katie was raised by a single mom who suffered from a severe mental illness. Her mother's mental illness resulted in Katie suffering from significant emotional abuse most of her life. I truly believe that it was Katie's plight that helped me conceive the parasite model. I know now how Katie's parasite blatantly played the "if only game". "If only I had someone to love me, I could believe that I was not damaged." I cannot tell you how many times Katie said that to me. Let us examine this more closely. Katie was convinced that she needed concrete proof in order to believe that she was not damaged. She wanted the impossible. She wanted someone to love her, even though she refused to love herself. Katie's therapy focused on this single aspect for more than six months. Eventually, she grew more accepting of herself. She did, in time, find someone to love her, and she was married. Because her new husband had difficulty with Katie being in therapy, Katie stopped her therapy. Approximately eight months after her marriage, she returned to therapy with another parasitic if only. This time, as you probably could guess, the if only was "If only I could have a child, then I would really know I am not damaged." It was at this point that I began to believe that abuse was a true disease, and Katie's disease was raging. No matter what I could do or say, she was back to believing she was damaged and this began to have a negative impact on her marriage. Intimacy with her husband, which had been positive, became cold and mechanical. She began to question his love. Therapy was going nowhere and she was frustrated beyond belief. One day, in a session, the parasite baited me. Unfortunately, I took the bait and said something that Katie perceived as hurtful. I immediately apologized, but the harm was done. She looked at me and said, "I am letting you down, and even you know I am damaged." I felt completely sick inside. During the next few days, I consulted with my colleagues, and I found myself saying to them, "This thing baited me, and I took the bait. This thing is intelligent, cunning, baffling, and powerful." That is how I came to develop the concept that abuse/trauma results in a parasitic disease. During the very next session, I continued to ask Katie to forgive my blunder. Fortunately, she did and we began to rebuild our therapeutic relationship. Within the next few weeks, I introduced Katie to the concept of the parasite. Perhaps it was her trust in me or perhaps it was the weight of Katie's tremendous pain; regardless of what motivated her, the concept of the parasite made perfect sense to her. Together, we set a new course for therapy. No longer would we end up attacking the parasite tentacle by tentacle, which I have said I believe is analogous to chemotherapy. We began to identify the parasite and directed therapy at radiating it, in order to force it to release its grip on the parts of Katie. Let me explain that last statement. Katie always kept a diary. I requested that she journal between sessions and bring this journal with her for us to review. In closely scrutinizing the journal, Katie was able to distinguish when the parasite was talking as opposed to when she was talking. This helped Katie begin to talk back to the parasite. There were times when her journal was pure Katie as we labeled it. She kept those entries in a separate folder. When she became aware of the parasite talking in her head, she would go back and reread the pure Katie folder. The fact that she was able to definitely curtail the parasitic thinking became quite empowering for her.

Eventually, Katie was able to embrace the fact that she was not damaged and began to accept herself for who she was. She worked at the intimacy with her husband and gave birth to a beautiful baby boy. Today, she would be the first to tell you that it was not giving birth that convinced her she was not damaged and not responsible for the abuse. By her own will and her own resilience, she convinced herself. When you attempt to ascertain what you need to do to heal yourself, remember Katie. Remember the answer lies in you.

You may ask the question, "Will this parasite ever be gone?" No. But you can shrink it to a point where it no longer creates pain. That is what I mean by radiating the parasite rather than using chemotherapy. And like many parasites, a significant portion of the parasite is excreted out of your body. A part of it can lie dormant. It can surface its ugly head every now and then, but you will now have new skills and abilities to effectively cope with the parasite.

# FOUR

# The Impact of Abuse on Development

Dr. Andy Carey and I collaborated to publish an article in the American Counseling Association's *Counseling and Values.* What was missing in our article were the concepts of the illness model and the parasite. Our original article concentrated on parent–child dynamics, with the parent as the abuser. Obviously, we know that the parent is not always the abuser. You know all too well who abused you. It might be that you suffered abuse/trauma at the hands of several individuals. Regardless of whom the abuser was and how you were connected to him or her, it was someone you trusted, and he or she violated that trust, and infected you with a parasite that continues to be excruciatingly painful. This chapter provides you with a greater understanding of what has happened to you and how a younger you adapted in order to survive. While it details a process of pain, it also demonstrates the vitality, the strength, and the resilience of the human spirit to survive. Armed with the knowledge of what and how some issues developed, and the knowledge that you are battling a parasite and not yourself, you can and will make your life different.

Magid and McKelvey (1989) studied and introduced "the concept of children without a conscience." They observed severe interruptions in development in the first one-and-a-half years of these children's lives and

Portions of this chapter were reprinted from Lemoncelli, J., & Carey, A. (1996). The Psychospiritual Dynamics of Adult Survivors of Abuse. *Counseling and Values, 40,* 175–184, by permission of the American Counseling Association. No further reproduction authorized without written permission from the American Counseling Association.

have hypothesized that these children suffer from a complete lack of bonding with another person. Their identifying this lack of bonding offers much promise in treating troubled children. Children who act out and exhibit negative behaviors at an early age might be considered lucky in the sense that their pain is being noticed. We can only hope that these children receive appropriate and sufficient treatment to aid them in their suffering. Nevertheless, we all know that the system that is supposed to provide treatment to these children or to any children or adolescents for that matter is stretched beyond the limits and is totally underfunded. However, Magid and McKelvey's theory does not account for those individuals who have seemed to survive abuse/trauma with a highly functional and intact conscience. These individuals appear to have taken on the role of the good child. In this chapter, I am referring to these individuals who exhibit the good child syndrome, which will be explained in a few moments.

The research regarding child abuse/trauma indicates that abuse typically begins very early in the child's life. This chapter demonstrates the impact of abuse on crucial child and adolescent developmental stages. For many individuals, some form of abuse did begin early in life. Yet, some individuals did not experience abuse/trauma until adolescence. If you experienced your abuse/trauma early in childhood, this chapter will be easier to understand. Regardless of when the abuse/trauma occurred, we need to be aware of the fragile nature of the child's or adolescent's ego. When abuse/trauma is experienced later in one's development, there is a significant amount of regression that occurs because of the fragile nature of the ego. I do not know when your abuse/trauma began or even what type or types of abuse/trauma you experienced. I do know the older you were when the abuse/trauma occurred, the harder it is not to hold yourself responsible. I want you to keep the case example of Danielle in mind. Remember that it was critical to her recovery that she does not hold herself accountable for the sexual abuse she experienced as an adolescent. Danielle was looking for someone to affirm her and to love her. She was looking for someone to trust. She was not looking for someone to molest her. You know the pain can be so overwhelming that you would almost do anything to ease it. I know for myself that pain clouds my vision and sense of reality. Your pain may have clouded your vision, but that does not mean that you must assume all responsibility.

In an examination of research studies concerning survivors of abuse/trauma, three concepts appear to be quite important in understanding the impact of abuse on development.

First concept: Appropriate and healthy parent–child bonding or attachment is a vital step to the child's early psychological health. Attachment lays the foundation for the child to develop a connection with another and simultaneously begin to formulate boundaries between the child and the parent. Physically holding the child close in one's arms and speaking in a gentle, caring, and loving voice are just a few things one can do to support healthy bonding and attachment. When the child does not experience these behaviors in a consistent manner, the child begins to display dysfunction. There appears to be a direct relationship between problems with attachment or bonding and dysfunction. It is safe to say, the more problems there are with bonding, the greater the child's dysfunction. Individuals who have been abused typically state that they have no desire for a relationship with the abuser, but there is still a need and usually an unconscious desire for some level of attachment. Emotional attachment with the parent or caretaker is of utmost importance to the child. An analogy of this is that an astronaut leaving the spaceship needs a lifeline connected to the mother ship. This lifeline provides the astronaut with the safety and security necessary to avoid floating aimlessly into space, where he or she will surely die. No healthy person wants to feel that they are aimlessly floating in space, just waiting to die. Bonding provides the child with a psychological lifeline.

Second concept: A critical aspect of development is the child's need and desire for consistency. Developmental psychology has long held that during healthy early childhood, a child develops a sense of egocentrism and almost a sense of omnipotence. When the child cries, someone comes to his or her aid. If the child is hungry, the child is fed. If the child is in distress, someone holds him or her and eases the distress. The important issue here is consistency, and the consistency reinforces in a healthy fashion the child's egocentrism. Unfortunately, abusive relationships lack consistency. Unconsciously, the child begins to assimilate that he or she is the cause of the inconsistency. This inconsistency only serves to provide the parasite with the necessary energy to both cause and maintain ego fragmentation within the child. When parents are inconsistent, the child experiences tremendous turmoil and anxiety. With dysfunctional and inconsistent parents, the child becomes entangled in the emotions of love and rage while desperately seeking to balance these emotions. Remember, we are talking about a child who does not have the cognitive capacity to rationalize his or her feelings. What is occurring is totally unconscious.

Third concept: The child is unable to maintain two different emotions simultaneously and, therefore, resorts to the third key concept known as splitting defenses. The concept of splitting enables a child to maintain some semblance of equilibrium or balance and a needed sense of attachment with the parents despite the inconsistency of the parents. The more dysfunctional the parent is, the more the child resorts to extreme methods of remaining attached. The child develops the notion that he or she is the problem. A contaminant, which is the parasite, has infiltrated the child's sense of self, the ego, and begins to fragment the ego. This fragmentation or this splitting appears to, for the moment, reestablish the child's equilibrium. This response allows the child to internally maintain an idealized, all-loving view of the parent. This inner fantasy view of the parent also enables the child to maintain the needed parental attachment for the child's sense of security and safety. However, this inner safety and security with the parent is maintained at the expense of the child's sense of self and self-worth. The child, now baited by the parasite, continues to blame the self for the bad that is occurring in the child's life. In addition, the longer this splitting occurs, the longer the child continues in self-blame and destructive self-views of himself or herself and the more these patterns appear in the child's relationship with others.

Faced with these inconsistencies of the parent, the child continues to attempt to make logical and rational sense in an environment where no logic or reason exists. This is where the parasite now takes over the child's ego by means of false internal statements that place the responsibility for the abuse/trauma onto the child. The parasite seduces parts of the child's self to wage war with the part or parts that are responsible for the abuse. The need for attachment only increases as the inconsistency continues. The terror, turmoil, and pain created by the abuse itself and the inconsistencies coupled with the need for attachment create a dynamic and dramatic bonding process. As this process continues, the child is baited or seduced by the parasite to internalize the source of his or her pain and create a dysfunctional bond with the abuser in order to create some consistency in the child's otherwise inconsistent world.

This bond can best be understood utilizing Berne's (1961) concepts of ego states. Remember his theory on the need for strokes or attention? Berne also postulated that three separate ego states exist in all humans. He referred to the ego states as Parent, Adult, and Child. However, these ego states do not typically correspond to the definitions we normally use when speaking of parent, child, and adult. According to Berne, the Parent ego state is the recorder of external events. The Parent has two separate parts: the Nurturing Parent, which is loving, kind, and compassionate, and the Critical Parent, which is negative, oppressive, and controlling. The

Child ego state is where feelings and emotions are recorded beginning from birth. The Child records the perceived external events and records the emotions or feelings associated with these perceived events. The Child ego state has three parts: (1) the Natural Child is the source of all positive feelings, (2) the Adaptive Child is the source of negative feelings, and (3) the Intuitive Child is a source of intuition and problem solving. The Adult ego state is more neutral and is concerned only with data and is devoid of feelings. It has been likened to a computer in that the Adult ego state stores and reports data. Let me give you an example. Suppose you were to tell your sister that she looked beautiful today. That would be a Nurturing Parent statement. You might expect her to smile, feel good, and say thank you. If that was your sister's response, it would be from her Natural Child. Just the other day, I remarked to a fellow faculty member, "You look tired. Are you okay?" Unknown to me that she was having a very bad day; she replied, "Thank you. You look sick." My statement was from the Nurturing Parent. Her response to me was from her Adapted Child. By the age of two, the child is able to internalize numerous recordings of experiences in his or her head. Simply observe a child at play mimicking what the child has heard and experienced. One of my crude responses to a mess used to be, "Man, this is a shit house." We visited my mother-in-law one day when she was housecleaning, and, of course, the room appeared quite messy. We were all appalled when our two-year-old son announced to his grandmother, "Man, this is a shit house." Our son was simply mimicking what he had heard from me. A child learns what a child hears, sees, and experiences. Given all the exposure to the Critical Parent of the abuser, the child begins to formulate his or her own oppressive and controlling Critical Parent. This Critical Parent evolves as an internal representation of the child's external realities. The Critical Parent within the child forms an alliance with and develops a bond with the actual abuser's Critical Parent. The bond provides the child with a basic sense of attachment and develops some consistency in his or her otherwise inconsistent world. This negative bonding, produced by the parasite, gives the parasite increased power and control over the child's sense of self. The child will be infected with more and more contaminants, which will provide the parasite with an enormous and continuous source of energy.

The noted psychologist Erik Erikson (1963) described a series of stages in a child's development. The first stage involves the child's need to develop a sense of trust. Dysfunctional bonding results in a basic sense of mistrust. The only thing the child can trust is that he or she will be hurt and that he or she deserves the hurt and pain he or she experiences. The next

Ericksonian developmental stage is autonomy verses shame and doubt. The child, influenced by the parasite, not only learns a sense of shame and doubt, but also dramatically internalizes these concepts. The child views the self as a source of his or her parent's pain and, therefore, the cause or source of the abuse. Both the child and the abuser parent become even more bonded as they unite to root out the source of pain and abuse. The child longs for the moment when he or she will eventually, with the parent's help, be freed from the part of the self that has caused all the pain and afterward achieve the intimacy he or she so desperately needs and desires.

The third year of life is recognized by many theorists as a critical year for the child. The child should no longer need to split the mental representations of the parent into the good parent and the bad parent. The child rather should be able to see the parent as one whole, and not the splits. According to Erickson, the child must also master initiative over guilt, which is his or her third stage of development. However, the abuse and the pain experienced by the child are far stronger than his or her initiative to achieve goals. The child sets, as a goal, victory over the pain and terror he or she continues to experience. The child attempts to end the abuse and inconsistency by somehow removing or exorcising the part or parts of the self that are responsible for the pain. As this insurmountable battle wages within the self, the child continues to experience turmoil, pain, and terror. All initiatives are aimed at disarming the bad child within or, in other words, stopping the abuse. However, all of the child's initiatives are met with defeat. The child continually assumes responsibility for his or her parent's moods, emotions, and behaviors. The child would do anything to please the parent. The child now takes on the role of a pleaser in order to reduce the parent's pain and displeasure believing that this will stop the abuse.

During the ages of three to five years, Erickson postulated that the next developmental stage or crisis is for the child to develop a healthy sense of industry versus inferiority. As the child continues to know only defeat in the child's attempts at reducing his or her pain, the child develops a deep sense of inferiority. Erickson suggests that it is at this point where the most fateful split in the emotional self occurs, the split between the potential for human glory and the potential for self-destruction. Because of his or her inferiority resulting from not being able to please the parent and subsequently the failure to control the parent's behavior, the child gives psychological birth to a fragment self that is committed to self-destruction. The parasite that has caused the fragmentation now is able to infect numerous parts of the ego. The parasite makes certain that the hostility the child experiences remains aimed at the child's sense of self. The bond between the abusive parent and child is strengthened. The child now envisions his or her own destruction as the only means of staying attached to the external world where approval and love are at best minimal and completely conditional. The child imagines that there is a source of badness within him or her and continually attempts to compensate for this badness. The child strives to regulate this badness by a commitment to self-punishment, self-debasing, and, if necessary, self-destruction. This aspect to development allows the parent's Critical Parent and the child's Critical Parent to become enmeshed as together they unite to destroy the child's perceived badness. The result is the formation of a greater sense of attachment for the child to his or her parents. The fragmentation, the conviction of a badness existing within and the guilt of being the cause of the pain for both the parent and the child, serves to force the child to strive for perfection as compensation for his or her inferiority. As the child strives for perfection, a paradoxical effect begins to emerge. The child, determined to achieve perfection, is forced to see even more imperfection within the self. This paradoxical effect produces a tremendous sense of inferiority within the child. It is at this point in development that the child's entire life becomes a paradox. The child is often viewed by the outside world as a model child. He or she is frequently praised outside the home and genuinely admired for his or her sense of responsibility, his or her work ethic, and his or her willingness to please others. This is what was referred to earlier as the good child syndrome. However, the child is never able to integrate this praise and admiration because the weight of what is happening at home is much more intense. Inside the home they are criticized, humiliated, battered, and sexually victimized. As the child struggles to destroy the perceived badness inside of him or her, the child is actually almost entirely suppressing, distorting, and destroying the innocent part of the self. These dynamics and the resulting emotions consume the child with a sense of inferiority, which will greatly impact the next Ericksonian stage of identity versus role confusion.

The child is caught in a love–hate world. For the child, the world is an endless double bind in that no matter what he or she does or does not do, the child cannot win. The child hates the abuse, the intolerance, and the pain but is completely convinced that he or she deserves the cruel and brutal treatment that he or she is experiencing. The child longs for love and approval but continues to feel unworthy of genuine love. The child is a victim of a negative self-fulfilling prophecy. The child attempts to make logical, rational sense out of his or her pain and horror, but as the child strives to make sense, where no sense can be made, the parasite reinforces the only logical explanation of his or her plight—that he or she deserves what is happening. The child is not worthy of respect and allows the self, as a people pleaser, to be used as anyone desires. Often the child believes he or she has no right to say *no* to anyone, for any reason. From the child's perspective, the rage that is felt must be suppressed, not only because he or she deserves what is happening, but also because the anger toward another is morally wrong. Morality and a sense of righteousness become new weapons for the parasite to use against the child. As the child continues to strive for perfection, he or she becomes increasingly aware of his or her imperfections.

In adolescence, the individual needs to develop a sense of identity verses role confusion, according to Erickson's theory. For the victim of abuse, the individual typically becomes enmeshed in self-destructive behaviors. Some individuals surface from their plight as suffering from various mental disorders, such as anxiety, depression, eating disorders, and cutting behaviors. However, the strength of the secrets typically prevents any intervention into the source of the problem. The adolescent, as in childhood, continues to be viewed with admiration, respect, and dignity. The parasite continues to block any absorption of these positive feelings by playing the "if only game". "If only they knew what a disgusting and horrible person I was, they would have no respect or admiration for me." This parasitic gaming prevents the adolescent from developing a true sense of identity. Rather, the adolescent appears to morph into whatever another person wants him or her to be, as opposed to who the adolescent wants to be. The adolescent really has no true sense of identity due to his or her feelings of inferiority. The adolescent survives the perils by identifying and compensating with good in hopes of eventually casting out the perceived bad or evil within the self. As he or she emerges from adolescence into adulthood, he or she externally portrays an excellent sense of goodness and model behavior.

As an adult, the individual continues the self-abusive process. Many marry abusive spouses who allow them to remain united in a common bond with someone who will aid them in destroying the parts of the self that are responsible for their plight. Unaware of the parasite that has infected him or her, he or she persists at expelling the truly innocent part or parts of the self. There is indeed a thing inside of him or her that needs to be excreted, but what needs to be excreted is the parasite and not a healthy vital part or parts of his or her ego. Regardless of marital status or vocation, a victim remains psychologically isolated and introspective. He or she is very capable of giving love, but cannot truly receive it and integrate it. He or she has barricaded parts of the self to protect the other parts from the bad or the evil. The end result of this isolation is that the victim is unable to psychologically absorb any positive affirmations or strokes. However, any and all negative defamations or strokes are completely absorbed and provide the parasite with a continual source of energy.

## SPIRITUAL DEVELOPMENT

Before we examine the spiritual development of victims of abuse/ trauma, it is important to define what is meant by spiritual. The American Psychological Association's *APA Dictionary of Psychology* defines spirituality as "(1) a concern for or sensitivity to the things of the spirit or soul especially as opposed to material things." *Webster's Dictionary* defines spiritual as: "(1) pertaining to the spirit or soul as distinguished from physical nature." Since both definitions seem to point to the soul and not religion, I then went back to the *APA Dictionary of Psychology* to define soul. Soul is defined as the "nonphysical aspect of a human being considered to be responsible for the functions of mind and individual personality and often thought to live on after the death of the physical body." So then, let me make it clear that when I speak of spiritual I am not talking about religion or religiosity. I am talking about the essence of who you are and your connection to a thing or being outside of you that helps to give your life meaning and purpose. This thing or being is a force greater than yourself and is a reflection of a goodness that exists in you. For some it may be God; for some it may be a Higher Power; for some it may be life itself; and for some it may be the belief that despite all the bad humans can do to one another, there exists a potential for doing good in all of us. I have been searching for a term that would be generic enough to include God, Higher Power, or any other source of Goodness in order for you to see that I am not speaking about religion, or doing any preaching. It struck me that perhaps the most spiritual people in history were the Native American Indians. The majority of the various nations of American Indians displayed an incredible spirituality. They saw the earth as sacred. They saw the rain as sacred. They saw life itself as sacred. And every sacred gift was given to them by the Great Spirit. I would hope that you and I could use the term Spirit to be inclusive enough to assist you in tapping into your spirituality. I like the term Spirit because it is devoid of a masculine or feminine identity, and it can be imaged based on your needs and where you are today. So from now on, let us use the term Spirit, which you can define as you see fit to represent God, Goodness, Higher Power, or your sense of Spirituality. I hope you can find a sense of goodness out there that will assist you with sensing the goodness inside of you. Please note that when speaking of a Spirit, I am not necessarily speaking about God, per se. Your Spirit may be a concept such as the wind on your face on a crisp and clear spring day, filling you with the fragrance of lilacs and the knowledge of the earth's rebirth. I am currently working with a young woman whose Spirit is an old Japanese maple tree that was planted for her by her beloved grandmother. Whenever this young woman is happy or sad, confused or troubled, she will sit under this tree and connect with her grandmother who she believes gave her a sense of goodness with which she can connect. Unfortunately, I do not know your connection to a Spirit, or a God, or a Higher Power. I do not even know whether you desire a connection to a Spirit. We will come back to this discussion regarding a connection to a Spirit and the role it can play in your healing later. I do know that many victims of abuse/trauma have significant difficulty with the concept of God and/or Higher Power. As we examine the impact that abuse/trauma has on the spiritual development of the child and/or adolescent, please bear with me.

The spiritual development of a victim of abuse/trauma parallels psychological development in that the process is highly adaptive but simultaneously very dysfunctional. Two key forces that play a major role in this process are, first, the transference of the parental image to the Spirit image and, second, the child's fixating on a mythical–literal stage of spiritual development. It is recognized that most victims of abuse/trauma have been reared in situations where the parents or caretakers typically adhere to the principles of the various faith-based denominations. In most religions, particularly the Judeo-Christian denominations, the image of Spirit as a parent prevails. It is natural then for the child reared in one of these faiths to develop concepts of Spirit based on their experience with earthly parents. During early childhood, not only is Spirit imaged from the child's parental experience, but also mythical notions about Spirit are developed. There is simplicity and security about this stage and the literal interpretations seem to fit a victim's black–white thinking. For the child, spiritual development is painful, frightening, and highly conflicting. In the child's mind, the Spirit is the parent who will do anything to make him or her good. The Spirit, like mommy and daddy, wants what is best for me and only punishes me because the Spirit wants me to be perfect. The child assimilates that like the parent, the Spirit will love them some day when they have rid the self of the bad or evil and become worthy of the Spirit's love. The relationship with the Spirit therefore necessitates more splitting defenses on the part of the child in order to maintain a connection to the Heavenly Parent. The self has been fragmented on both spiritual and psychological levels. The drive for perfection takes on a new dimension: "not only do I need to be perfect to have the Spirit love me, but I need to make myself perfect in order to attain salvation."

As the victim of abuse/trauma emerges into adulthood, he or she maintains the childhood notions and fears about the Spirit. The Spirit, in a mythical way, remains vengeful and conditional. In the victim's need to make sense out of his or her senseless experiences, he or she frequently views his or her pain and suffering as a special blessing from the Spirit. In the Judeo-Christian traditions, as well as other religious traditions, the victim holds firm to the principle of guilt and punishment, and often views the pain and suffering endured as a pathway to salvation. The victim takes the position that if any good occurs, it is because the Spirit alone has done this and it is not due to the individual's cooperating with the Spirit. Similarly if any bad occurs in his or her life, it is solely because of his or her own flaws and behaviors rather than any other possible explanations. As a result, these mistaken attributions serve to reinforce the need for self-punishment and self-debasement.

Trust is obviously an essential component of faith and spiritual development. Because victims lack trust, their spiritual development remains impeded and they remain stuck in the immature stages of spiritual development. They remain spiritually bound in this love–hate relationship with the Spirit, demanding perfection of themselves. There is a part of him or her that is enraged by his or her sense of abandonment by the Spirit. Simultaneously, he or she is terrified by this anger for fear of the fact that the Spirit will even send him or her more punishment. This cycle of rage and fear escalates the victim to relentlessly strive for perfection and the pleasing of others. He or she is guilt ridden about doing anything for himself or herself as this is typically viewed as selfish. The victim is overly concerned about fulfilling the wants and needs of others, terrified by his or her anger, and depressed by the emptiness he or she feels inside. He or she desires an intimate relationship with the loving and beneficent Spirit but fears the nonexistence of this beneficent Being. His or her perceived unworthiness and inability to trust prevent any level of intimacy with this Spirit from being experienced. Unless there is an intervention in the spiritual dimension of the victim, the wounds from the abuse/trauma will not truly heal. Effective treatment often becomes thwarted in the spiritual dimension because many therapists neither investigate nor attempt an intervention into the sacred spiritual domain. At this point, I am sure you have many questions: "Is he saying that I must believe in the Spirit in order to achieve healing? Is he saying I must start praying or join some kind of religion?" The answers to these questions are absolutely no. What I am saying is that if you profess to have a belief in the Spirit, you need to work on rectifying the relationship with that Spirit. If the Spirit thing is not something for you, that is your perfect right. But I am asking you to work at a connection between you and a force or source of Powerful Goodness outside of you. The source of Goodness will afford you a reflection of the Goodness that I know exists in you. A Goodness that you must come to believe exists in you.

My experiences tell me that you might be asking the same questions that have been asked of me. For example, "Where was this beneficent, loving Spirit when I was getting the hell beat out of me? Where was this Spirit when my mother killed my baby sister? Where was this Spirit when I was being degraded and humiliated day after day? Where was this Spirit when it seemed like the whole school turned on me and I was being bullied? Where was this Spirit when a clergy person forced me to touch her? Where was this Spirit when my pain became intolerable?" The truth of the answer is "I really don't know." Perhaps my image of the Spirit is too humanized. But I do believe that this Spirit was right there with you experiencing your pain as no human could ever experience it. I believe this Spirit was right there with the Christ as he hung nailed to a cross and when he cried out, "Why have you forsaken me?" I know that it is very difficult for you to find Goodness in the midst of all that you have suffered. If you are enraged with your Spirit, trust that this Spirit understands and would validate your right to feel this rage. If you are so enraged that you really cannot deal with the Spirit right now, so be it. I can well appreciate your position. I hope you can take my validation of your feelings and allow yourself the right to what you feel.

My work with clergy and victims of abuse/trauma alike has afforded me an opportunity to appreciate that the Spirit they have come to believe in is internalized on two levels. The cognate Spirit is the one most individuals talk about, preach about, and the one they truly want to believe exists. It is almost as if they idolize something they have never experienced but want so much to experience. The affect Spirit, on the other hand, is the one we relate to and experience on a relational level. These concepts are more often than not very different representations of the Spirit. I have had patients who talk about a loving, forgiving, gentle, and beneficent Spirit. They can and do make this Spirit very attractive and most approachable. But when they really become honest with themselves and me, the affect

Spirit is harsh, cold, demanding, vengeful, and unforgiving. Because of their experiences with their abuser, they continue to make the split between the cognate Spirit and the affect Spirit. And the affect Spirit is the one they relate to, the Spirit they are supposed to trust. How can a being like this give any one comfort? It cannot, and it does not, and that is the problem.

It is my firm hope that you are beginning to sense why it is so important to include the spiritual aspects as part of your healing. When I was in training in the 1980s, psychologists did not speak about religion, spirituality, or the Spirit. It was as if these subjects were taboo. Within the past 10 to 15 years, more and more psychologists have come to believe that the spiritual dimension of humans can be a key factor in promoting mental health. In order to appreciate a human being, to study and treat a person as a whole, we need to assess the physical, psychological, and spiritual aspects of the person. While psychologists are not medical doctors, we typically obtain a full medical history on every patient. Why would we not obtain a spiritual history? If this chapter made you uncomfortable, I am truly sorry. However, what has been stated in this chapter is based on how the parasite twists and distorts the image of the Spirit until the Spirit is nothing more than another abusive agent in the lives of the abused. If this is not the case for you, then you are truly blessed, and it is essential that you tap into this strength and resilience to aid you in healing your psychological self. However, always keep in mind that the parasite is cunning, shrewd, and powerful. It has shattered your trust in yourself and any goodness that might exist in you. As it blames you, it is distorting your image of the Spirit and you begin to blame the Spirit. If you find the parasite has twisted your sense of the Spirit into simply being another source of pain, please do something about it. Talk to your therapist. If that is not comfortable for you, then find a trusted person who can assist you with spiritual direction.

I would like to share with you a portion of my own struggle with the Spirit. There was an event in my life at the age of 20 that twisted my affect Spirit into a conditional, vengeful, and vindictive Being. It would be inappropriate to share the details, but there were some very understandable reasons why my affect Spirit became twisted. All the theology courses and all the homilies that I heard had very little impact on altering my perception of the Spirit. It was a very lengthy conversation I had with my dad and subsequent spiritual direction that helped me to alter my perception and my relationship with the Spirit. Growing up, my dad was not very religious. He did not go to church much, but he prayed daily. I have come to appreciate that while my dad was not religious, he was a deeply spiritual man. Dad was not highly educated since he finished only the seventh grade, but he had incredible wisdom. Dad had what I refer to now as raw wisdom. One day I was watching our children. I had recently been notified that I had failed my second attempt at the challenging psychology licensing exam. (By the way, I did pass the exam on the third trial.) Dad, knowing that I was quite upset, came for a visit. I began lamenting about the exam and I was blaming the Spirit for my failure. I asked my dad, "Why would the Spirit allow this to happen to me?" Dad's response was kind but stern. He said, "Son, when bad things happen, do not blame the Spirit. You know, son, you and your sister have done things that have hurt me. You and sis have done things to make me very angry. Yet, no matter what you have done, or could do, nothing would make me so hurt or angry that I would give you cancer or heart disease or make you fail your test. No, son, I would not do that and I am just a fallible man who loves his children and wants them to be happy. Do you think the Spirit could love you any less? Can you think of anything that your children, Mark or Mauri, could do to you that would make you just want to hurt them? You forget that evil exists. Evil thrives on our pain. Evil thrives on our misunderstanding of the Spirit. Remember, son, the Spirit did not crucify Jesus. Evil and evil men did that." What my dad said to me made sense. It is my hope that what he said makes sense to you. Many times my patients have asked me to share my image of the Spirit. I analogize the Spirit to be similar to Home Depot or Lowe's. The Spirit, like Home Depot, has everything we could possibly need to build a home. The Spirit will even deliver the materials to your site. The Spirit will put people—electricians, plumbers, and masons—in your life to help you. But the Spirit does not lay a block, sweat a pipe, or drive a single nail. That is all up to us. I challenge you to build your house. The Spirit will grace you with what you need to accomplish your goal. If you are furious with the Spirit, give your fury to the Spirit. The Spirit will know what to do with it. If you cannot trust the Spirit, talk to the Spirit about your mistrust. The Spirit already knows. Above all, work at never allowing a human, a religion, or a parasite to come between you and your Spirit.

Before concluding this chapter on the psychospiritual aspects of development, it is essential that we revisit and take into account the age you were when you were abused. As previously stated, if Danielle was reading this chapter, she would say, "This does not pertain to me at all because I was 18 when I was sexually abused." If Sally, another patient of mine whom you will meet later, was reading this chapter, she would say something very similar. Sally would say, "I was 11 when the abuse occurred. I did not have many of the issues you pointed out in early childhood." You may have made the same or similar statements. I have presented to you a chronological order to the abuse. The research literature does tell us that most abuse begins early in a child's or an infant's life. You may have been abused by a neighbor at age five and therefore might justifiably be saying, "This does not explain my situation at all." Soon after I began theorizing about the disease and specifically the parasite, I questioned whether the developmental theory would be of any use to my patients. After introducing the parasite to new patients, there was a realization that regardless of when the abuse began, or the type of abuse it was, the developmental difficulties remained the same. The only differences I could uncover were the differences in the degrees of difficulties depending on the age of the person when the abuse occurred. No matter what type of abuse was experienced or at what age the abuse occurred, the abuse/trauma has significantly similar results. It appears that abuse/trauma causes significant regression in the child or adolescent. Perhaps this is because the ego in childhood and adolescence is not fully developed and, therefore, quite fragile. Quite possibly, it is because of the parasite's ability to fragment the ego, developmental issues such as trust, which had previously been resolved, become unresolved. For some individuals who were abused later in childhood or adolescence, the disruption in trust of the self and others can often be greater because the parasite plays the "I should have known better" game. You will need to confront this irrational belief in order to reduce the responsibility you feel for the abuse/trauma. This is where your connection with the Spirit becomes critical. Do you really believe the Spirit agrees that you should have known better? Do you really believe the Spirit holds you responsible for your abuse/trauma? Certainly, a rational part of you knows that you were not responsible. The Spirit in you is powerful. You need to begin to trust in yourself and the Spirit. Together, you and the Spirit are much more powerful than any parasite.

# FIVE

## Some Issues to Assist You in Therapy

### BEING IN THERAPY

We have already discussed to some degree how therapy can assist you in healing from the disease of the parasite. My hope is that you are already in therapy and that your therapy has begun to truly help you heal. Perhaps you have found or will find some things in this text that you believe would augment your therapy. Share these sentiments with your therapist. Perhaps you are feeling frustrated and stagnated in your therapy sessions. You need to discuss your frustration with your therapist. Remember it is not your job to please your therapist. Rather it is your job, with your therapist's help, to continue in the process of healing. Remember that healing is not an event but truly a process. This process will have ups and downs. The parasite will use both the ups and the downs against you. Change is definitely a frightening process. As stated before, you need to embrace the fear and to acknowledge it with your therapist. The parasite will tell you in the downswings, "See you really are a failure. You are even failing at therapy. How disgusting is that?" And in the upswings the parasite will say, "You think you are really better? Remember how many times you have failed before. The higher you go up, the further you fall and you have always fallen." You and your therapist together need to identify how the parasite is continuing to play with your thoughts and your feelings.

Let me give you a detailed example of how the parasite played with one of my former patients. Beth was a 46-year-old married woman who was a devout Christian with high moral standards. Her history revealed a significant struggle with her father who "drank too much and was emotionally abusive," and a mother who was emotionally "neglectful." When she was 16, she married a very gentle and loving man who was significantly older than she was, just to get away from her parents. The couple had three children and, for the most part, she was a stay-at-home mom. Despite the trauma of her abuse, Beth was able to establish a very strong, trusting, and intimate relationship with her husband. However, Beth suffered from of a severe panic disorder that prevented her from traveling more than five miles from her home. As a stay-at-home mom, the panic disorder really did not cause significant difficulties in her relationship with her husband or her children. She was able to make excuses as to why she could not travel. With the children grown, her husband now wanted her to travel with him more extensively. Her panic disorder escalated and became a source of significant difficulties between Beth and her husband. As we began treatment, it was obvious that Beth had long suffered alone and struggled with the parasite. Dynamically, Beth's husband filled the void she experienced from both her father and her mother, thus proving that she was lovable. Her relationship with her husband called for her to address the issues of her childhood. She found the concept of the parasite to be extremely helpful, and within a period of four years she was discharged from my care.

Ten years later Beth returned to counseling. Her husband was stricken with a very aggressive form of Alzheimer's disease. She was filled with anger and frustration watching this gentle loving man turn into someone who did not even recognize her. She had reported that for the last five years she had cared for him at home. It was becoming obvious that her husband was going to need nursing home care. She was completely devastated. She was furious with the Spirit because now when she was able to enjoy traveling with her husband, the Spirit gave him this horrible, crippling disease.

Keep in mind that Beth and her husband had enjoyed an active sexual intimacy. Obviously, the sexual intimacy, or any intimacy for that matter, had long since passed. In one of our sessions, Beth announced to me that she was going to have an affair. To be honest, I was taken aback by this decision. I asked her whether we could spend some sessions exposing the pros and cons of her decision. She agreed and we spent several sessions examining the consequences of a possible affair. It appeared to me, and I told Beth, that it seemed as if she was simply striking out with her anger at the Spirit. I asked her to think about how she would feel afterward. It became obvious to both of us that having an affair would be parallel to emotional suicide for Beth. What was helpful to Beth was the sanctioning of her right to be angry with the Spirit and to bring that anger to the Spirit. In a subsequent session, she said, "Maybe I need to forgive the Spirit." I said nothing, but watched as some of the fury melted from this woman's face. What an empowering notion! Instead of asking "why me," she started asking "why not me?" What a remarkable and powerful shift in perception! Please know that in this situation I was not making a moral judgment regarding her initial decision to have an affair, because that would have taken away her autonomy. I simply served as a sounding board for her in her continued struggle with the parasite. Beth receives all the credit for struggling against the parasite and preventing an emotional disaster. The parasite manipulated her into thinking that an affair would make her feel better. In essence, striking back in this fashion at her Spirit would have only served to distance herself from the Spirit. Due to her high moral standards, she would have experienced tremendous shame and guilt after having this affair. It would also, parasitically, have given credence to her biological father's message that she was not lovable.

You may ask, "Will my therapist tell me how to get well?" You can see from the example of Beth, the answer is no. You hold in your hand the keys to your healing. A good metaphor for a therapist is that the therapist functions as a global positioning system. You decide where you are going and where you want to arrive, and the therapist helps you navigate to your destination. One of the principles of counseling and therapy that I hold most firmly is that a person walks into my office with the problems or issues in one hand and the solutions in the other hand. My job, and your therapist's job, is to believe in you and to believe you have the answers. Then we work at transferring that belief to you that you indeed have the solutions. You and your therapist need to work at blowing the fog away that prevents you from clearly seeing the issues and the solutions. Your therapist will need to look to you for the answers of what you need to do to heal. The clarity is not there yet, but be assured the answers are there. Sometimes the parasite will confuse you with erroneous possible solutions. Some of these solutions may need to be challenged—not to say you are wrong, but because sometimes the parasite will contaminate a potential solution just as in the case of Beth, and in the previous case of Danielle who wanted to confront her abuser. The parasite baited both of these women into viewing possible solutions that might have been disastrous. This is why it is so important that you work with the therapist you believe in and you trust. If you are not in therapy currently, I would ask you to seek out a reputable, licensed therapist who has some knowledge and experience in treating survivors of abuse/trauma. You may need to do some shopping until you find the right person for you. If you find that you are not feeling comfortable with the therapist, discuss this with the therapist. If that does not work, find another therapist. You can give up on the therapist; just do not give up on you and the need for therapy. Please remember, no one goes it alone.

Over the course of the past 10 to 15 years, counseling and psychotherapy has shifted from a dysfunction focus to a strength-based focus. When my patients would enter therapy, it was very easy for them to tell me all the things that were wrong about them. When I would shift the focus to positive things, and asked them to tell me five positive things about themselves, they were typically at a loss to tell me anything positive. Instead of focusing on all the things you dislike about yourself, you need to begin to refocus on all the positive things about you. You may be saying to yourself, "There really is nothing positive about me." Stop for a minute. If that were true, you would have achieved negative perfection, and that is a total impossibility. No human is capable of either positive or negative perfection. Therefore, you need to look deeper and closer inside of you and ascertain some positive aspects of your personhood. The parasite will fight you on this. The parasite may insist there is nothing positive about you, or the parasite may tell you that anything positive about you pales in light of your damaged and disgusting personhood. Do not listen to the parasite. I do not know you, and yet I can tell you something positive about you. Despite all of your suffering, you have worked very hard, perhaps even too hard, not to inflict pain on others. Even when you may have been tempted by the parasite to inflict pain on others, you turned that anger inward and inflicted pain on yourself. Another positive is the fact that you have carried this terrible burden for so long. This struggle demonstrates the amazing strength you have inside. You have attempted to heal without really knowing how to bring about true healing. Is that not documented evidence of your resilience? You can clearly see there are indeed positive aspects of your personhood. Now, with this strength and resilience, and a clear pathway to healing, you can become a true survivor of abuse/trauma, and not remain a victim.

## SEMANTICS OR GENUINE THOUGHT PATTERNS

You may recall the Gestalt theory that we discussed earlier in this text. As part of his theory, Fritz Perls (1969) also theorized that words we use are often genuine reflections of our thought patterns. It is also thought that the words we use are reflective of our view of ourselves and our world. What is interesting about these concepts is the fact that these thought patterns and subsequent views of ourselves and our world can, and often do, lead to self-fulfilling prophecies. You may not know exactly what is meant by a self-fulfilling prophecy. According to the *APA Dictionary of Psychology,* a self-fulfilling prophecy is defined as "a belief or expectation that helps to bring about its own fulfillment, as for example, when a person expects nervousness to impair his or her performance in a job interview, or when a teacher's preconceptions about a student's ability influence the child's achievement for better or worse." Obviously there are both positive and negative self-fulfilling prophecies.

Think about this for a moment. Is there a difference in the statements, "I will try to heal my pain" versus "I will heal my pain"? At first glance, you may say no, there is no difference. Please look closer. The word try appears to lack commitment and therefore may imply failure. It is very important that we begin to become aware of the terms we use as we begin this journey of healing. If you were my patient, you would be asked not to use the word try. Rather, you would be asked to use the phrase, "work at." Be assured that I would not impose goals on you. That is not how therapy works. You and your therapist will collaborate on the various desired outcomes that you establish for healing. However, once you commit to a goal, I would ask you to phrase that commitment in terms of "I will work at achieving…" You see here we are committing to a process and therefore are more apt to develop a positive self-fulfilling prophecy. When your therapist asks you did you work at your goal, even if you did not fully achieve the objective, you can respond, "Well, I worked at it." You see if you worked at it, you were successful. You can take that success and build up your ego and began to integrate your strength rather than your weakness.

There are numerous words and phrases that are problematic to you taking control to recover, because the parasite will use these words and phrases to negatively shape your thought patterns. Take the word *deserve.* How many times have you heard the phrases, "I deserve your respect," or "I deserved a normal childhood," or "I deserve a better job." *Deserve* is a problematic word. If said enough, the individual develops a thought pattern of entitlement. Sure, your abusive parent may have wanted your respect, but what did he or she do to earn it? Certainly, you needed a normal childhood, but what can you do to get it back? An individual may need a better job, but he or she must work at getting a better job. If you just go through life letting the parasite say to you that you deserved a normal childhood, you will get stuck at attempting to get back the childhood you never had. This type of thinking will only result in you becoming angrier and more frustrated, and the parasite will feed off of this anger and frustration. The parasite will then bait you into using this anger and frustration in self-destructive, self-defeating behaviors. As we discussed earlier, the key to your taking control to recover is to accept what has happened and what cannot be undone. In a logical, rational world, it would seem to make sense that people get what they deserve. However, you know all too well this is not a logical and rational world.

I have a wonderful wife and we have two great adult children. In comparison with other families, have we done something special to deserve them? I think not. On the other hand, have I done something so terrible that I deserve to lose them? I hope, before the Spirit, that I did not or ever will not. Infants are born addicted to drugs their mothers ingested during pregnancy. Do you think these infants deserve to come into the world addicted? Talented, gifted people like athletes make millions of dollars playing sports. Did they do something to deserve those talents? Did you deserve to be abused? People have issues, situations in their lives—some good, some horrible. Rather than getting stuck in the "I do deserve this" or "I do not deserve this," suppose we alter the focus and work at coping with what we have, good and bad. In chapter 2, we examined the serenity prayer and we discussed accepting what we cannot change. Here again, I am reminding you that we cannot change what has happened to you. And yet, here is this tremendous opportunity to take what has happened to you and truly experience the strength and resilience you have. You, somehow, were able to get through all that pain and suffering. You need to grasp that strength and resilience, no matter what the parasite tells you, and resolve to work at taking control to recover.

Other problematic words are *worthy* and *justice*. As human beings, are we ever worthy of having someone love us? Are we ever worthy to have the Spirit love us? Does a child need to be worthy in order to be safe from abuse? You know the answer to these questions is no. Several years ago, I treated a 23-year-old woman who was molested by a neighbor at the age of 14. In order for her to make love to her husband, she had to spend at least an hour showering before she could even consider intimacy. This was, typically, in addition to the three or four showers she would normally take during the day. The parasite told her she was so dirty and disgusting that this was the only way she could go near this man who truly loved her. Regardless of the time she spent in the shower, she never felt worthy of being intimate with him. Do you see the futility in this? She was unable to feel worthy on the outside because she felt so unworthy inside. When someone loves you and cares about you, accept this love graciously. Do not let the parasite play the worthy game with you. What kind of justice would truly help you heal? Can the perpetrator of your abuse/trauma take it back as if it did not happen? Can the perpetrator give you back your childhood? Does true justice really exist in this world? Suppose you were to embrace the fact that these concepts, such as deserving, worthy, justice, are rarely present in this world. Perhaps they do in an afterlife, but I really do not see them reliably present in this world. But if you allow the parasite to play its games, it will cause you to persist in seeking these concepts and thereby inhibit your taking control to recover.

You may remember Tammy's story and how she was told by professional hospital staff to just get over it. Many of my patients have said to me, "I just need to get over this." Perhaps you have said the same thing to yourself. The phrase "get over it" is incredibly problematic. Unfortunately, I have no idea what that phrase means, and neither did any of my patients. So in reality, my patients found themselves working toward a goal that had no meaning to them. Do you know what it means? How does one get over the loss of their childhood? How does one get over the abuse/trauma? You see, in life, we work through events, situations, and/or experiences. The phrase "working through" involves a process, while "get over it" appears to be an event. You need to focus on the process of healing, rather than the event of healing. If the parasite or other people in your life have been saying to you, just get over it, please do not buy into this problematic phrase. Focus on the process of healing, not the event of being healed.

Albert Ellis, in his counseling theory, believed that there are other problematic words that presuppose unrealistic and irrational expectations. These words are *shouldas, couldas, wouldas* (Murdock, 2009). "I should have never trusted her. I should have known better. I could have made her happy, and then she would not have abused me. If only my father would not drink, he could be a loving father." Do you see the unrealistic expectations we place on ourselves and others? How could a child have known not to trust the teacher? How could a child control a mother's happiness? How does the child stop a father from drinking? Where is it written that a child should never trust a father, a neighbor, a teacher, a coach, or a clergy person? These problematic words lead to unrealistic expectations for you. And the parasite will use these unrealistic expectations to maintain your responsibility for the abuse/trauma. Is any human born with a crystal ball?

Does any human, much less a child or adolescent, have that kind of control in life? Of course, the rational side of you is saying no. You need to begin to use your resources to refute the irrationality and the nonlogic that the parasite plays against you. You had no control in the abuse/trauma situations, but you do have control as to whether you choose to accept the parasite's illogical and irrational statements. Ellis would say, "Do not 'should' on yourself." It appears to me that he certainly has a valid point.

You may ask, "Where is he going with this? Why is he so focused on semantics?" It is because the parasite will use many of these words and phrases (and others like them) to play its game in your head and your heart. You need to be cognizant of these words and the subsequent games the parasite will play with you. You need to listen to the chatter in your head and you need to work at becoming more rational regarding your expectations of yourself and others. The words and phrases actually can become red flags for you in that they will actually signal that the parasite is at work baiting you into irrationality. Allow the red flags to be your ally and use the rational part of you to immediately begin refuting the parasite.

## YOU HAVE A CHOICE—THERE IS REAL POWER IN THAT CHOICE

For the longest time, the parasite has created an ultimate dilemma for you, and you have bought into that ultimate dilemma. The dilemma is the fact that you can stay in your pain and turmoil and therefore allow the parasite to continue to have control over you. Or you can risk admitting that you are powerless to change the past and begin to take control over the parasite. However, the parasite has you terrified to engage in a battle that the parasite tells you that you cannot win. There is an old quotation that says, "The devil you know is perhaps better than the devil you do not know." The parasite is using this as a game to play you. You know that you want to be rid of the pain and turmoil that you are in right now. This pain and turmoil represents the devil you know. At the same time, you are frightened and reluctant to experience the unfamiliar pain of identifying, radiating, and excreting the parasite. This fear and reluctance represents the devil you do not know. Will you commit all your psychological and spiritual resources not to allow the parasite to consume one more day of your life? Will you commit to working at this process until you are free from the parasite's control? You may be thinking that you do not have a choice, and that is exactly what the parasite wants you to think. You find yourself caught between the devil you know and the devil you do not know. Both sides of this dilemma are terribly frightening. But you do have a choice and there is incredible power in that choice. The parasite is playing you. It is telling you that you have to get rid of it, and it is attempting to bait you into a war with it, as it tells you that you cannot win this war. Nothing, no parasite, no therapist, no family member can force you to work at eliminating the parasite. You may be thinking that you do not have a choice because the alternative is to allow all the pain to continue and for you to remain miserable. But, you see, that is a real choice. Let me give you an example. Suppose an individual is struggling with an alcohol addiction. He is admitted to the hospital with severe pancreatitis. After this very severe illness, he is warned by his doctor that his next drink could kill him. It might appear that the man really does not have a choice. But the reality is he does have a choice. He can begin a long and difficult road of recovering, or he can continue to drink and eventually die. That man has a choice, and so do you.

## ALTERING PERCEPTIONS

Psychology tells us that there is a reciprocal process between our cognition (thoughts) and our affect (emotions or feelings). If I think about my dad who passed away a few years ago, I might feel very sad. As I continue to experience this feeling of sadness, more thoughts begin to pass through my mind. I may begin to think about how the horrible disease of Alzheimer's reduced this man who was bigger than life to a child who did not even know me. Each cycle of thoughts and feelings, feelings and thoughts establishes momentum. Given a few moments in this cycle, one can easily begin to feel as if ones' head is spinning. Yet, when I shift my thoughts and begin to think about many of the things he taught me, and I remember his goodness, I began to feel gratitude for having him as a dad. When I began to think about the task ahead of me in completing this book, I began to feel quite anxious. My parasite begins the "what if" games, and the anxiety increases. To some degree, this reciprocal process of thoughts and feelings is analogous to being on a spinning ride at an amusement park. The first few cycles are tolerable, but after a period of time, it feels like you are out of control.

We have discussed to some degree how our history and our perception of that history tend to color our view of ourselves, others, and our world. If your history and the perception of that history taught you that you were damaged, you will perceive yourself as damaged no matter how good you may look or feel today. However, because perceptions are learned, they can be altered by new learning. You can learn and process new and more accurate information in order to alter your perceptions. Nonetheless, you must be willing to make the necessary adjustments in your perception. Truly, it is easier said than done. But it can be done if and when you chose to do it.

You might well remember Danielle's situation. Danielle took control and started to heal when she began to alter the perceptions of herself. She chose to relinquish much of the responsibility for her abuse, and she chose to see herself as fragmented but not damaged. You may be asking how she altered her perceptions. First, after a very long and difficult struggle, she accepted what had happened to her. Second, she chose a path toward healing, which required her to alter her perceptions of herself and the abuse. Right now, a metaphor may help. We are on a bus trip to New York City. It is a cloudy, dreary February day. As the bus traverses through the streets of Manhattan, we see hordes of people. The streets are somewhat dirty and littered. Some of the people on the streets appear hurried; some appear happy, while others appear sad. The bus drops us off at the Empire State building. We decide to walk up 10 flights of steps. When we finally arrive on the 10th floor, we pause to look out the window. The city begins to look quite different. Suddenly it is nicer, cleaner, and less congested, but remember, it is the same city. We decide to climb to the observation deck. It is a long, hard, almost exhausting walk, but we accomplish our objective. When we look out once more at the same city, it looks totally different. Now we have three different views of the same city. All are real, but all are different. Which perception do you choose? Do you choose to maintain your first perception of the city, or do you choose an alternate perception of the city? You might be saying to yourself, "Okay, I understand the point he is making, but you cannot tell me the process is that easy." You are most correct. Is not that easy, but it is possible. What you need to do in counseling is somewhat similar to the earlier example. If you truly desire to alter your perceptions of yourself, you can and you will. When you alter the perception of yourself, you will begin to think and feel differently. But in order to alter these perceptions, you must climb the stairs. There are no elevators. The climb will be difficult and sometimes exhausting, but when you reach the floor you need to be on, the climb will be more than worth it. When you realize that you are not responsible for the abuse/trauma, that you are not damaged, and not broken, you will be able to give yourself the respect and dignity you need. This will, in turn, take much of the power away from the parasite. Once you begin to take the power from the parasite, you will begin to experience a decrease in the self-abasing statements. This then results in a subsequent decrease in self-defeating behaviors, which in turn allows you to feel even more respect and dignity toward the self. Now, instead of the negative self-fulfilling prophecy, you have a positive self-fulfilling prophecy.

A key element in altering perceptions is to first identify the rational, logical parts of your ego versus the parts of your ego that have been infected with irrational and illogical notions by the parasite. This will require you to challenge both your thoughts and your feelings. You know too well the responsibility you bear for the abuse/trauma. Have you ever really challenged the rationality and the logic behind your acceptance of this responsibility? How could Greta logically and rationally take responsibility for her baby sister's death? Greta believed that if she maintained the responsibility for her sister's death, Greta was also maintaining the reality of her death. This concept of holding on to the responsibility in order to maintain the reality of the abuse/trauma is easily understood by the majority of my patients. While I can appreciate the concept, the logic and rational thinking eludes me and my patients agree. There is an incredible twist that the parasite creates in our emotions. There is a significant difference between the emotions of sadness, guilt, and shame. It appears to me that the parasite actually collapses these emotions into one, thus creating guilt and shame, when there needs to be simply sadness.

The *APA Dictionary of Psychology* defines sadness as "an emotional state of unhappiness ranging in intensity from mild to extreme and usually aroused by the loss of something that is highly valued, for example by rupture or loss of the relationship." The *APA Dictionary of Psychology* defines guilt as "a self-conscious emotion characterized by a painful sense of having done (or thought) something that is wrong and often by a readiness to take action to undo or mitigate this wrong." On the other hand, the *APA Dictionary of Psychology* defines shame as,

> a highly unpleasant self-conscious emotion arising from the sense of there being something dishonest, ridiculous, immodest or indecorous in one's conduct or circumstances. It is typically characterized by withdrawal from social intercourse, or distracting the attention of another from one's shameful action, which can have a profound effect of the psychological adjustment and interpersonal relationships. Shame may motivate not only avoidant behavior but also defensive, retaliative anger. Psychological research consistently reports a relationship of proneness to shame and a whole host of psychological symptoms, including depression, anxiety, eating disorders, subclinical sociopathology and low self-esteem.

As you can see from these definitions, sadness, guilt, and shame are very different emotions. However, in the human experience, these emotions feel somewhat similar and can be easily confused. By accepting the guilt and the resulting shame for your abuse/trauma, the parasite is able to manipulate you to continue to attempt to undo your history. More tragically, accepting the guilt and shame affords the parasite the power to hold you responsible for your abuse/trauma. You need to redefine what it is that you feel. Is it really guilt? Is it shame? Is it both? Did you, in fact, do something wrong, or did the parasite simply manipulate you into believing you did something wrong? The sadness you hold as a result of the abuse/trauma is a difficult burden in and of itself. However, as you well know, the guilt and shame you bear are a much heavier burden, and the guilt and shame result in you holding yourself accountable and responsible. You need, over time, to continually reexamine and eventually begin the process of relabeling what you truly feel. While I cannot tell you how to feel, I can ask you to logically reexamine the feelings of sadness versus guilt. If we examine the serenity prayer and begin to accept what we cannot change, then we can focus our courage on changing those things that can be changed. Logically shifting from guilt and shame to sadness is something we can change and will be an incredible source of healing.

It is clear that we can understand Greta's need to remember her baby sister. It is logical and rational that she feels incredible sadness. However, it is critical that Greta recognizes sadness does not imply guilt or shame. And if there is no guilt or shame, there is no responsibility. Many of my patients are currently working on truly separating these three emotions. Once you make this distinction, you will be astounded by the progress you will make in your healing. If you consider some of the key points in chapter 4, you will see how easy it is for the parasite to collapse these emotions in the mind of the child or adolescent. Because we humans are incapable of true abstract thinking until late adolescence, the parasite is able to easily collapse these emotions. Through this process the parasite is able to maintain your feeling of responsibility for your abuse/trauma, and this is a powerful source of energy for the parasite. I would ask you to consider this next thought. We have discussed the concept of splitting defenses in a child's development. You need to use this ability to split against the parasite. You need to split the difference between remembering and responsibility. You need to split the difference between the reality of what happened and the responsibility for what happened. You need to hold on to the pain of the reality of what happened and begin to let go of the responsibility for what happened. When you distinguish logic from illogical and rational from irrational, you will be equipped with other ways for you to identify when the parasite is talking to you and when you are talking to you. It is a learning process of listening closely to your internal monologues and dialogues. The closer you listen, the more you will recognize you versus the parasite. It is definitely a process of trial and error. There are times you will succumb to the parasite. It is critical to understand you cannot win every battle. Be patient and forgiving with yourself when you lose a battle. Forgiveness and patience will immediately take away the energy from the parasite. You cannot win every battle. Keep your vision on winning the war. That is what is critical.

## ARE YOUR FEELINGS OBJECTIVE REALITY?

In this section we will begin to tie two significant issues together. We have already examined the fact that there are no bad feelings or emotions. Remember that we discussed there are positive and negative feelings. What we have not discussed about feelings is the fact that a feeling can be very real to us internally and yet have little or no rational external validity. If we were sitting together talking, you might sit there as an adult person and tell me that you feel like a dirty, disgusting, little child. That feeling is certainly real to you on the inside. That feeling must be validated. You have a right to that feeling. However, that feeling, as strong as it may be, has no objective reality. While I would validate your right to feel that way, and certainly tell you that I can appreciate what you feel, I would also tell you that this feeling has no objective reality. In reality, I do not see the child. I see an adult, and I do not see anything dirty or disgusting about this adult. If I gave you a mirror and asked you if you saw a dirty, disgusting child, I am sure you would undoubtedly say, "I see an adult." This is objective reality, and while you continue to feel the way you do about yourself, the feeling is real only internally and not externally.

I know that my telling you what I see does not make your feelings go away or even subside, and I respect that. Feelings do not just go away. That is not the way we humans function. But feelings can be altered if we are willing to alter our perception of ourselves or our situations. Again, it is your choice. Do you choose to alter your perceptions and thereby alter your feelings? Do you choose to see this adult who is neither dirty nor disgusting, or do you choose to continue to see a dirty, disgusting little child? If you do not choose to continue to see yourself as a child, then you need to begin to work at seeing something different. We need to perceive this adult person who has demonstrated incredible resilience. As you began to alter your perceptions of yourself, your negative feelings regarding the self will begin to subside. Feelings are real to the person, and they identify where the person is emotionally at a given moment in time. But while feelings are very real internally, they do not necessarily have any external reality. If you said to me, "I feel like a piece of garbage," I am not going to put you in a plastic bag and put you on the stoop for the garbage collector. Similarly, if you said to me, "John, I feel so good today I feel as if I could fly," I am not going to allow you to exit my office out of the fourth-story window. You are not garbage, and you cannot fly. Both the negative and the positive feelings are your reality internally, but these feelings are not the external reality. Just because you feel guilt and have assumed responsibility for your abuse/trauma does not make this the external reality. If you choose to alter your perception of your abuse/trauma, you will begin to feel less and less responsible. Within this process, as you began to feel less responsible, you will begin to alter the guilt you feel, which is irrational, and begin to feel only sadness, which is rational.

The parasite has been, to this point in your life, very powerful. The parasite has manipulated you to feeling guilty regarding your abuse/trauma and is thereby able to hold you accountable and responsible for the abuse/trauma. The parasite has also created a distorted perception of who you are based on how you feel. Perceiving yourself as a dirty, disgusting little child rather than a competent adult has allowed the parasite to maintain control over you. Take a moment with me and imagine two identical twins who are approximately two years old. One of the twins has just had a bath, and his mother has sprinkled him with baby powder. He looks precious and smells angelic, and he is giggling and cuddly. It would seem to me that neither you nor I would have any difficulty picking up the child and hugging him very warmly. Now, I would ask you to picture the other twin. He has a terrible cold, a snotty nose, and some of the mucus has crusted into his hair. He has poop in his pants and up his back. He neither looks pretty nor smells pretty. In addition, because of his cold, he is feeling miserable and really whiny. It is not as easy for you or me to pick up this child and cuddle him. Nevertheless, this is our challenge. We need to recognize how much this child needs to be held and needs to feel loved. The parasite has distorted your image of your child part and has baited you into believing if you are able to get rid of the child you will undo your abuse/trauma. You need to come to terms with how much your perceived dirty, disgusting child needs you to love him. When you start to accept this child part and hold the child close to you, you will begin to perceive the beauty of your child. You will actually begin to see the beauty of you. It was the parasite that distorted your child part's beauty and created the negative feelings you have toward your child part. It was the parasite who created the notion that this child part was ultimately responsible for your abuse/trauma, and if you could get rid of it or him, you could feel good again. The parasite has been saying, "He got you into this: get rid of him." What you have not done, but truly need to do, is to love this part of you, which you have perceived to be a dirty, disgusting child. The child part of you is innocent and an essential part of you. Attack the parasite and begin to drive the parasite out of you, not the child part out of you. When you stop listening to the parasite, and work at integrating this child part and the other parts of you, you are, in effect, radiating the parasite.

## DID I HAVE A RIGHT TO A HAPPY CHILDHOOD?

Over the last 25 years, many, if not all, of my patients have said to me that they believed they deserved a happy childhood. If they did not use the word "deserved," they may have used the phrase "had a right to." Many of my patients believed they should have had a happy childhood. If you look back to the section on semantics or genuine thought patterns, you will recognize that all these words and/or phrases are what I have already referred to as problematic words and phrases. These words and phrases, and subsequent thought patterns, provide the parasite with an incredible source of energy and power. The parasite will utilize this power to maintain your misery and simultaneously keep you stuck in your misery. "You deserved a happy childhood and you did not get it. You got screwed. You are damaged. So there is really nothing left for you to do but to be miserable for the rest of your life." As we discussed in the section on spiritual development in chapter 4, the child or adolescent is attempting to make sense out of the incredible pain were truly no sense can be made. However, the child or adolescent is incapable of comprehending that her situation makes no sense and uses faulty logic to make sense out of nonsense. The parasite, using this faulty logic, plays various parts of the self against one another to ensure fragmentation of your ego. In this way, the parasite keeps you at war with yourself. The parasite may have baited you to be at war with life itself. You have given up on hopes and dreams because there seems to be no use for you to hope or dream. It feels to you that life just will not let you win, no matter what you do. This sense of hopelessness and helplessness affords the parasite even more energy to continue its stranglehold on the parts of you. The parasite may have also baited you into being at war with the Spirit. "The Spirit allowed this to happen. Surely, the Spirit could have stopped it." What might be even more detrimental is that it seems to you that for some reason the Spirit selected you personally to experience the immense pain and suffering of abuse/trauma. To you, the Spirit is nothing more than a real SOB that cannot be trusted. What is almost paradoxical is the fact that all this time that you have been at war with yourself, life, and/or the Spirit, the parasite, creating the intense ego fragmentation, has been getting stronger and you are feeling weaker.

You and I both hope that every child will have a happy childhood free from abuse/trauma. You know all too well that this is not the reality found in this world. There is nothing anyone can do or say to make your childhood up to you. There is nothing anyone can do or say to give you back your childhood. By holding on to the notion that you had a right to a happy childhood, your efforts of undoing your history, does indeed, keep you locked in the past without a sense of present or future. This is how the parasite is able to manipulate you into remaining a victim. No matter what words you use—deserve, right, should, guarantee, or expectation—they are all problematic. These words or phrases become thought patterns that the parasite uses well to keep you from working at moving on with your life. Please notice, I did not say get over it. Rather, I said work at moving on with your life. You see there is something you can do today to begin working at taking the power back from this parasite. There is something you can do today to work at minimizing the self-victimization, which is a result of your abuse/trauma. There is something you can do to make sure the parasite does not take one more minute of your life. You need to stop just existing and waiting and hoping for someone or something to fix you. You are *not* broken. You need to work at becoming a survivor.

## DID I LOSE MY INNOCENCE? DID I LOSE MYSELF?

Adults can take many things away from a child or an adolescent. Adults could take the child's or the adolescent's happiness, trust, safety, self-esteem, and hopes. The adults can and do destroy the childhood and the adolescence. Adults can and do take the very life of a child or an adolescent, but I do not believe anyone can ever take their innocence or fully destroy their sense of self. There is an incredible resilience that I have spoken about before that exists in children and adolescents.

Many of my patients have told me that their innocence was taken from them. It feels that way to them and that is their internal reality, but as an external reality, I do not really believe that abuse/trauma takes away a child's or adolescent's innocence. That is part of the problem. If you were sexually abused, the parasite has been telling you that your innocence, your virginity, and your purity have been taken away. That is simply not true. The abuser took away your childhood or adolescence, portions of it or all of it. However, no abuser can truly take away your innocence or your purity.

Allow me to use an analogy to make my point. The majority of religions in today's world have what are believed to be holy artifacts: a book, a symbol, blessed water, bread, or a place of worship. In Catholicism, Catholics believe that the consecrated piece of bread is the body of Christ. For Catholics, this is the Holy of Holies. Suppose an evil person took a consecrated Host and desecrated it. Through this desecration, did this evil person destroy the essence of the holiness of the Host? Did this person take away the Host's innocence, purity, or goodness? I believe he did not. He violated the Host. That is true. He perhaps altered the Host's outward appearance. However, the internal form remains unharmed. The Host maintains its purity and its holiness. According to the Muslim religion, the Koran is a very sacred book holding the teachings of the Prophet Mohammad. If an evil individual desecrated this holy book, would it not still, regardless of the desecration, be a sacred book? Does the desecration take away the holiness? In both situations, the internal form remains unharmed. In a similar fashion, you may have experienced, as a result of the sexual abuse, some physical scarring in the genitalia. However, your true internal form remains unharmed. It is the parasite that wants you to believe you are damaged. You are not damaged. You have been violated, but you have not lost your innocence or your purity. You need to believe that you continue to maintain your innocence and your purity and take back the power, both from the abuser and from the parasite.

For the longest time, you have probably felt and continue to feel that the abuse/trauma has destroyed your sense of self. Perhaps my telling you that you have been infected with the illness of the parasite may have, at some point, only served to confuse you all the more. The fact that you are reading this book is in all actuality proof that you have not lost yourself. Yes, the abuse/trauma, and the resulting infection of the parasite, has created much confusion regarding your sense of self. The abuse/trauma has negatively impacted your sense of trust of self, others, the world, and perhaps even the Spirit. The parasite has used this lack of trust of self to create the fragmentation we have been talking about throughout this text. The fragmentation coupled with the lack of trust of self results in the feeling inside of you that you have lost yourself. While that feeling is real to you inside, it has no external reality. We need to convince you and you need to accept and convince yourself that the real you is still very much present and alive. You may be asking, "Can someone lose the self as a result of abuse/trauma?" Unfortunately, the answer is yes. Some individuals choose to allow the parasite to invade their soul and thus consume them. It is quite likely that the individual or individuals at whose hands you suffered your abuse/trauma chose to allow the parasite to consume their total being. You, on the other hand, have chosen a very different path. You have chosen not to permit the parasite to enter your soul and consume the essence of you. No matter where you are in the struggle with the parasite, you are to be most highly commended for hanging in there and not allowing the parasite into your soul. In your struggle and in your confusion, you may have abused yourself, but you never allowed the parasite to bait you into abusing another. This is one more positive aspect of who you are as a person. Embrace the parts of you that are confused. The parasite wants you to destroy the parts so that it can enter into your soul and then, subsequently, destroy the self (ego). Once the parasite accomplishes this, it will then be able to replicate itself in another by baiting you to abuse another individual. The parasite that you have been infected with through the abuse/trauma has taken an incredible toll on your childhood and adolescence. Do not let the parasite take anything else. Please believe what I am telling you and hold on to the notion that your innocence, your purity, and your soul are very intact and remain inside you. You need to love the parts of you that you have perceived as a dirty, disgusting child. He may look dirty, or she may seem disheveled and disgusting. The child part might be very angry, and this part of you has reason to be, because you have attempted to expel it from your ego. However, when you truly embrace the child, you will perceive exactly what I have been telling you. Your child part, and therefore you, is innocent, pure, and psychologically intact. You are not damaged.

## HOW DOES ONE EXPLAIN DYSFUNCTIONAL PARENTS?

I am not sure we can really explain dysfunctional parenting. Neither you nor I want to believe any parent would bring a child into this world just to abuse or traumatize the child. I must confess that I do not want to believe in a Spirit that sends children into this world just to suffer abuse/trauma. True, the Spirit knows what will happen, but that does not mean the Spirit ordains the abuse/trauma of children or adolescents. To accept that the Spirit actively wills that some children are destined to suffer abuse/trauma is completely incongruent with the goodness and the all-loving nature of the Spirit. The majority of all religions hold the premise that humans have been afforded the concept of free will. There appears to be a powerful and cunning polarity to the Spirit, and this polarity is evil. For the better or worse of the human existence, humans have the power to choose between good and evil. We both know that there are some very sick, perhaps, even evil, people out there. However, I am sure we want to believe that most parents bring children into this world with the best of intentions. But as the saying goes, "the road to hell is paved with good intentions." Good intentions are not sufficient to produce good parenting. We recognize that no parent is perfect. Unfortunately, the reality is that some parents are just better than others. Some parents are psychologically ill. That is not said as an excuse, but rather it is said simply to state a reality. Some parents participate in evil. Some parents just plain suck as parents. Your parents actively chose to participate in evil. If you were not abused/traumatized by your parents, then it was your abuser who actively chose to participate in evil. We do not know why; we simply know it happens. Life is unfair and it is not systematic. There seems to be no rhyme or reason. If I were born with Down syndrome, would there be any rhyme or reason for this? Genetically, we probably could explain it. But why does a mother give birth to one child with Down syndrome and subsequently give birth to two normal, healthy children? Why does one parent struggle with recovering from alcohol or other drugs and work at being a good parent, and another parent succumbs to the addiction and abuses her child? I do not know that we humans will ever make sense out of it, but we keep attempting to make some sense out of it. Maybe that struggle to make sense out of life eases our fear of the unpredictable roll of the dice nature of life. Perhaps a metaphor will help us better understand poor or bad parenting. This metaphor may seem odd to you, so I ask you to just bear with me.

Imagine parenting to be similar to an amphibious landing on a hostile beach. It is June 6, 1944, during World War II, and the Allies are attempting to launch an assault on the Normandy coast. You see landing crafts (parents) coming from large transport ships (the Spirit) and on the landing craft are the soldiers going into battle (children). The mission for each landing craft is to get its troops safely onto the beach. There is a great distance between the large transport ship (the Spirit) and the stress and the stress of life (childhood and adolescence) and the beach. The landing craft hover around large transports (gestation) and eventually are given the signal to head toward the beach (birth). But as they speed off toward the beach (which in reality is adulthood), numerous obstacles get in the way of their mission. Some landing crafts get blown up miles from the beach. The troops in the craft did not stand a chance. An example of this would be Greta's little sister. Some troops get dropped off a half-mile offshore with all of their equipment (the baggage of abuse/trauma) weighing them down. They put up a mighty struggle, and as they get their heads above water, they see some other landing craft get right onto the beach delivering their troops without a scratch, not even getting wet. I am sure the troops who were dropped off a half-mile offshore (perhaps you) might say, "Son of a bitch, why me? Why was I not that lucky?" Regrettably, I would be forced to say to them and to you, "I do not know." But I do know this: Wherever you were dropped off and whatever obstacles you encountered as you approached adulthood, that is where your war has started, and if you do not start moving forward, you are going to drown. You are going to get psychologically torn apart by the parasite. Your war started somewhere way offshore. Your abuse/trauma has caused you to swim for numerous years just to get to the beach. Your parents or your abuser prevented you from arriving safely on the beach. You are wounded and you are very tired but you are not damaged, and that is a key essential difference. The parasite will tell you that you are damaged. It will tell you that you were marked with the big D on your forehead and that you were marked from the minute you left the transport (Spirit). You are not damaged goods. You do not have to have a big D on your forehead.

There are two faulty parenting issues that I would like to share with you. The first is how many parents attempt to relive their own childhood through their children. In essence, these parents remain caught with the illusion that they can somehow recapture their childhood through their children. An example of this would be a mother, who throughout her childhood and adolescence had hoped for and wished for popularity with her peers. She now has a daughter who is somewhat shy and retiring but is quite a beautiful young lady. She is also an excellent student. Does the mother accept the daughter for who she is or does the mother push her daughter to become the person the mother wished she could be? This is nothing short of subtle abuse. The mother is negating the person her daughter is and essentially telling the daughter that, as a daughter, she is not good enough. It takes only a few subtle messages for the parasite to pick up on the daughter's failure to please her mother. This failure to please, and the message that she is not good enough, is enough for the parasite to begin wreaking havoc in the daughter's ego and will essentially cause many of the same symptoms overt abuse causes.

Fathers are equally guilty in this domain. An example would be for a father who was short in stature and frame but always dreamed of being on the high school football or basketball team. The father has a son, who, by age four, the father is pushing into all forms of sports. The son has every piece of baseball, football, and basketball equipment. However, the son is not very interested in sports. The son is quite studious, is reading way beyond his age level at age four, and desires to take piano lessons. The father is furious. His son is not going to be a sissy and take piano lessons. Instead, the father enrolls him in a gym so the son can take basketball and baseball lessons. Unfortunately, because the son neither desires, nor has the talent to perform athletically, the son begins to incorporate feelings of failure. No matter how hard he attempts to please the father, nothing seems to be working. How long do you think it will take the son to incorporate into his ego, the feelings of failure as an athlete and more critically his failure to win his father's approval? How long will it take the parasite to infiltrate this young, healthy boy and create enough fragmentation in the boy's ego to affect the symptomatology associated with abuse?

The second issue that I have heard so often in my clinical practice is the belief that parents hold that they both loved and treated their children in an identical fashion. The reality of this statement is that this is utterly impossible. I believe parents attempt to be fair and love their children in a similar fashion and perhaps even to treat them in a similar fashion. However, as most parents will admit, their children are very unique persons and quite different. We also must take into account the importance of perception that we discussed in detail in other chapters. Because the child is a unique individual and perceiving the acts or actions of parents differently, their relational experience with their parent or parents is quite different. If we use the example of Danielle, whose parents, by Danielle's perception, favored Alice, I would expect Danielle's parents to say, "We don't know what happened, we treated them the same and loved them the same." However, Danielle's experience and her perception, which is her reality, are very different. It is critical that parents realize that they can strive to be fair and firm and love their child as much as possible, but they will both love and treat each child somewhat differently. Parenting is the most important job any human can take on. Unfortunately, children do not come with instructions. Even more unfortunately, parents are fallible humans. In order to be the best parent one can be, one must recognize and embrace his or her own human frailties and how they can impact parenting and their child or children directly. A parent needs to celebrate the strengths, talents, and qualities of their child and assist the child to develop those qualities to the fullest no matter how different they might be. What a parent must refrain from is the temptation to relive their childhood through their children and from the temptation of creating a "mini me."

The parasite has been telling you for a long time that you are damaged goods. You need to dispel this notion. No one took your innocence and no one took your purity. They can and did violate your body physically and/or sexually, and they can and did violate you psychologically. But they cannot and did not violate your soul. Your soul is where your innocence still prevails; your soul is where the essence of you, fragmented as it may be, still prevails. The parasite wants your soul and if you choose to allow it, the parasite can penetrate your soul by scratching away and slowly destroying the essence of who you are. Once you are no longer you, it will take your pain and bait you to abuse yourself continuously and/or abuse those around you. It will bait you into actively seeking something that no one can give you, your childhood. We cannot get that back for you. You asked me what you need to do to heal. Because no one can give your childhood back to you, one positive thing you can and need to do is to grieve the loss of your childhood.

## GRIEVING THE LOSS OF YOUR CHILDHOOD

Grieve your childhood and/or adolescence. The parasite will tell you that you can get it back. It will also develop a faulty scheme to manipulate you into attempting to get it back. No matter what the parasite tells you, you cannot get it back. You cannot be a five-year-old again. You cannot, in a sense, go back to the transport and relive and rectify your journey to the beach. I know I am being redundant here, and I ask you to bear with me because the parasite has been and continues to be most redundant regarding the capturing of your childhood. So many of my patients found themselves stuck here for many years before they began to truly accept the reality. Throughout this text, you have heard me say, over and over, that we need to accept the things we cannot change. You know somewhere deep inside of you that this is what you need to do, but you do not want to do it. I truly respect that because I would not want to do it either. Regardless of how much you do not want to accept your reality, I am urging you to choose to accept it. Your childhood needs to be mourned, but in your grief and in your mourning, there is the hope. You now have the realistic hope that no one, no abuser, or no parasite, can take away another minute of your life because you are now the adult trooper. You are on the shore and you are on your feet, and you can choose to heal, and when you choose to heal, you will.

You might be familiar with the stages of grief and bereavement. If you are, then this will be a simple review. If you are not familiar with the stages, then this may prove very helpful. In 1969, Dr. Elisabeth Kübler-Ross published a book titled *On Death and Dying*. In that book she outlined five different stages that individuals experience during grief and bereavement. Notice that the author uses the term stages and not steps. The concept of steps connotes that a person is going up or down steps, and once he has made it to a particular step, he usually just moves on toward the next step. Similar to many other concepts we have already discussed in this text, the concept of stages implies a process. An individual might today be on the third stage and find himself back on the first stage by tomorrow. Like so many issues necessary for the process of healing there is a continual ebb and flow. The first stage is denial. The *APA Dictionary of Psychology* defines denial as "a defense mechanism in which unpleasant thoughts, feelings, wishes, or events are ignored or excluded from conscious awareness. It may take such forms as refusal to acknowledge the reality of the terminal illness, financial problem, an addiction, or a partner's infidelity. Denial is an unconscious process that functions to resolve emotional conflict or reduce anxiety." Denial acts as a buffer to the psyche and certainly you can see why you and so many other people have remained at this stage for quite some time. Initially, denial appears to make it easier to cope with the situation. However, at some point in time, we must accept the reality of our situation. Dr. Ross's second stage is anger. Once we accept the reality, we then begin to engage in the "why me" type questions. The more we asked the questions, the more intense our anger becomes. The third stage is bargaining. "If only my mother would ask for forgiveness, I might be able to heal. If only I could have stopped by mother, my sister would still be alive. If only my father did not drink, he would have never physically abused us or molested me. If only I could have found a way to make my parents proud, they would have never ridiculed me or said any of those so hurtful things about me." And the list could go on. Certainly we can understand how bargaining would play such a major role in abuse/trauma. The fourth stage is depression. My experience tells me that this is the stage where many people begin to seek treatment. When the depression and/or the anxiety become so burdensome, individuals who have been abused begin to seek out treatment. Perhaps for many, this becomes their salvation. I hope you have entered treatment long before this stage, but if not, there is no time like the present to seek out the help you need to understand and heal. The fifth stage is acceptance. I do not think I need to talk about this stage simply because I have been talking about acceptance throughout this text. Just remember that acceptance is a stage in a process and it is not an event where once you arrive you never go back. That is just not how healing works. As much as I have been redundant regarding acceptance, be prepared for the redundancy regarding patience with yourself and the healing process.

You may have spent a great amount of time moaning about you childhood. But lamenting or moaning is not really grieving. Do you hear the difference between what you may have been doing and what I am suggesting you begin doing? What I am suggesting is that you work at accepting the loss. You may have been told by others or by yourself to stop moaning and to just get over it, and get on with your life. Is that what I am saying to you? The answer is definitely not. You already know how I feel about the phrase "just get over it." And I am not saying, "Stop moaning about it." You and I may moan about some things that have happened to us for the rest of our lives. I do not know if you could ever get over your abuse. I do know that you can begin to work through your abuse/trauma.

Recently, one of my patients brought to my attention a concept that I had completely overlooked. (Oh well, as least I have acknowledged the fact that a clinician's best teachers are his clients.) Lonnie is a 50-year-old, single, never married, Caucasian professional woman. She and her four siblings have suffered immense physical and emotional abuse at the hands of her biological father. The father is 78 years old and in very poor health but in Lonnie's words, "he is still a mean, self-centered, vicious person." Lonnie describes that her mother is a rather frail woman who stayed in the marriage to provide as much protection to her children as possible. Lonnie's mother was also reportedly a victim of the father's physical and emotional abuse. For some unknown reason, Lonnie's mother never saw divorce as an option. I had asked several of my patients to comment on parts of this manuscript. This is in part some of Lonnie's comments: "The process of grieving and guilt. Maybe more on this. I have spent a lot of time trying to get back my childhood and trying to get a father, a real father. Most of the time just led to some sort of increased depression and that led to more self-abuse. I have spent most of my life grieving the loss of my father, which is why I believe I will not grief his physical death. Some real acceptance of my abuse/trauma came this past Christmas and has been reinforced with my nephew's serious illness. I believe only my father's physical death will provide me the ability to visit my mother more and will provide me with true acceptance. Unfortunately the time I have lost with my mother is similar to the loss of my childhood and is also something that I can't get back. When the time comes that I must bury my mother, I will not only grieve her but I will grieve the time he took away from us."

I could not have said it any more powerfully than Lonnie. What is also important to keep in mind regarding Lonnie is that she has committed to working through the grieving of her childhood and her father, and that she has a definite hope that she can and will work through this process. It is Lonnie's wish that you will also have this hope and begin your own grieving process. I do not know how much better the grieving process will get, but I do know it gets easier. Even though some things may not get all that much better, it truly does get easier to cope because you are working through it. But you must continuously cope. Am I saying that by grieving the loss of your childhood or a parent or parents you will completely accept this loss? Perhaps someday you will, but the important point is that you need to work toward some level of acceptance. In examining the stages of grief and bereavement, we have already discussed the fact that they are stages, not steps. You do not just arrive at acceptance. You work toward a level of acceptance. That is as good as it gets. Today I can accept some things better than I did yesterday. Tomorrow I might not accept anything. It fluctuates. When you have a sense of the Spirit and a sense of the goodness about yourself, it becomes easier to accept the fluctuations. Go back to the section on spiritual development, which you have read in chapter 4. You are a perfectionist and you want to do this perfectly. That unfortunately is not possible for you or any of us. We are all merely human and perfection is beyond our grasp.

Since I do not know your specific history, it is impossible for me to assess the particular aspects of your abuse/trauma. It may seem to you that your entire childhood and adolescence was permeated by your abuse/trauma, and that may be the reality you need to cope with in grieving. For some of you, there are possibly some positive aspects of your childhood and adolescence. If that is the case, I would implore you to hold on to those moments in time as treasures that can provide you with much hope. As we have discussed in chapter 4, the abuse/trauma necessitated a younger you to create numerous splits regarding yourself and your world. Until now the parasite has been able to use those splits against you. Now you need to take this adaptive skill and begin to use it for your own healing. Even if you believe there are no positive aspects about your childhood and adolescence, I would ask you to reexamine this belief and determine whether there are moments in time that you can split away from the abuse/trauma. This might be very difficult for you, but I know it is not impossible. This is something that I have asked every patient of mine who had suffered abuse/trauma. So many of them were astounded by the number of positive aspects they were able to split off from what they perceive to be a completely horrific childhood and/or adolescence. You may need your therapist's help in this regard, but I assure you it will be worth the effort.

## THE HUNT FOR THE EVIL

Early in my career of working with individuals who suffered from abuse/trauma, and long before I had theorized about the parasite, I began to notice that these patients seem to be playing some kind of game with me. The game might be called, "You think I am a good person, but wait until I tell you this about me." I now know that the parasite was baiting them into playing this game with themselves and with me. This game revolved around the core belief or the Adlerian basic mistake that there was something inherently bad or evil in them that caused the abuse. I now label the game—the hunt for the evil. For example, I was working with a young woman named April who had been sexually abused by her biological father from the age of three. The abuse stopped when she was six years old after her mother caught the father in the act of abuse. The mother immediately divorced her husband and petitioned the courts for sole custody. The custody battle dragged on until April was 13 years old. April testified before a judge regarding the sexual abuse. After testifying, the judge said to April, "Young lady, fathers do not do those kinds of things to their little girls." But the judge did grant sole custody to the mother. After about eight or nine months of working with April, I began to notice how she would twist her body into a particular position on the couch in my office. It seemed like a terribly uncomfortable position. After weeks of noticing this seemingly uncomfortable position, I asked her if she would like to sit somewhere else in the office. She declined and said, "You do not know this, but I am just a terrible person." It probably took us two or three additional sessions for her to tell me the reason she was sitting in that particular position. It was because she could not bear to look at the picture of my children that I had on a corner of my desk because she felt so jealous of them. April was convinced that I would think she was a horrible person if I knew how jealous she was of my children. She admitted to me that she really did not like my children even though she had never met them. April saw me as a caring father. She wanted a caring father and not the biological father who had sexually abused her. I told April that I thought this was a completely normal and natural response. Why would one not be normally jealous of something that someone else had?

I realize that in some religious denominations jealousy and/or envy are held as a violation of the Spirit's rules. If one looks to define jealousy and envy, they are very similar. A certain amount of envy or jealousy is quite normal. As we have so often discussed, the feelings that one has are not bad or evil. What I would call destructive envy is behavioral and that can be viewed as aberrant. If you just bought a beautiful, brand-new black Lexus, with black leather interior, I might be quite envious or jealous of you and your car. This is normal. Suppose you were standing on the street next to a really fancy restaurant. You are hungry and have absolutely no money or credit cards with you. You are also quite lonely. You see a couple walking into the restaurant hand-in-hand laughing. Do you wish that was you? Are you a little jealous or envious? Do you think you are evil because you feel this way? This is just normal functioning. Destructive envy or jealousy, on the other hand, is where one takes it to the point that if I cannot have it, you cannot have it either. So I take a key and scrape your brand-new Lexus. That behavior, not the feeling, is where we transgress against humanity and the Spirit's laws. Going back to April, she eventually was convinced that her jealousy did not make her a bad person, and we worked through her transference. However, her parasite continued to play the hunt for the evil game for quite some time.

The hunt for the evil is the parasite saying to you, "If they only knew about your abuse/trauma, they could not possibly like or respect you." Unfortunately, the parasite does not play this game just in therapy. The parasite has played this game for a long time and has caused you to keep your abuse/trauma a secret. This hunt for the evil game is a process we need to examine in detail. If you are in therapy and have confided in your therapist, you have already begun the process of taking some of the parasites power away. Obviously the parasite has convinced you that you are damaged goods and you are responsible for what happened. The younger you, the child or adolescent, attempted to make some logical sense out of the horror of your abuse/trauma. Of course, it does not make sense. Yet, you continue to look for something within the core of you as being inherently bad or evil. The parasite has continually baited you with the notion that if and when you find this bad or evil in you then you will be able to explain the abuse/trauma. Subsequently, when you find the bad or evil, then the abuse/trauma will make sense. Believe me, it will never make sense. You may need to play this game for a period of time. It actually may help you reveal some of the incredibly painful things that have happened to you. You and your therapist need to understand that this is a process you need to go through in order to truly heal. In sexual abuse/trauma, perhaps one of the most poignant issues is when a person says, "I wanted him to touch me; I wanted to feel special; and I needed to be loved." These represent the core fears for many victims of sexual abuse that perhaps they invited the abuse. Believe me, you did nothing to cause or invite the abuse. It is normal for us to want to be touched, to be loved, and to be held. I have never heard a victim say I wanted to be touched like that. In fact it is the reverse. "I wanted to be touched, but not there, and not like that." Perhaps you enjoyed being special to your abuser during the time you were being abused. You may have even felt some arousal in the genitalia. This is biologically normal. It does not make the abuse your fault and it does not say you either enjoyed or wanted the abuse.

If you are not a victim of sexual abuse/trauma, these next few statements may not be very pertinent to you, so please bear with me. Because for those of you who were victims of sexual abuse/trauma, there are some key issues we need to consider. We need to appreciate what is normal human functioning. Is it normal for a four- or five-year-old little boy to be touching his genitals? Of course it is. Is it normal for a little girl? Believe it or not, it is. You know what? It feels good. Contrary to Freud's notion that children are getting sexual pleasure by touching the genitalia, children are simply getting pleasure. Do they know they are masturbating? The answer is of course no. But again we need to appreciate the fact that the body is responding as it is programmed to respond. Even at an older age, if a woman's body is being touched against her will, the body might still respond with some sensations, some lubrication, and so forth. The body is responding: the body does not know it is being abused. The mind does. You were most likely saying, "This is wrong. This should not be happening." And you are right. You did nothing to cause the abuse/trauma.

With other forms of abuse/trauma, you may have done things that you knew would result in you being either physically or emotionally abused. For example, you may have stayed after school and played a game of basketball with your friends even though your father told you to come directly home and cut the grass. You know if he finds out, he will beat the crap out of you. And he does find out, and he does beat the crap out of you. Does that mean you caused the abuse? Absolutely no, it does not. In a healthy situation, your father might be justified in some sort of discipline for disobeying him. Your behavior does not justify his beating the crap out of you. You did not cause this abuse. You may have forgotten to study for a test and received a very poor grade that requires your mother's signature. When she sees the test paper, she begins the verbal barrage that is humiliating, degrading, and excruciatingly painful. Did you cause this abuse/trauma? Nothing you did or said can justify the violation of your boundaries that you experienced.

The parasite will play on your confusion and will convince you that you are inherently bad or evil and therefore responsible for the abuse/trauma. In this hunt for the evil, you and your therapist need to work together and examine in detail many of the aspects of your abuse/trauma. This process provides you with an opportunity to flush out those aspects. The doubts you may have about being responsible are typically where you believe the evil lies. You may also think that some of your feelings are an indication of the evil that lies within you. You may feel jealousy toward your therapist's children. You may feel love toward your therapist because the therapist is the first person who has ever given you undivided, positive attention without asking anything from you. You may have strong feelings toward your therapist, maybe even sexual feelings. Given the nature of the therapeutic process, these feelings can often occur, and they are considered quite normal. Of course, it is unethical for both the patient and the therapist to act on these feelings because the therapist is duty-bound to protect you in your vulnerability. Remember these feelings, positive or negative, are simply an indicator of your humanity.

The paradox in the hunt for the evil game actually needs to be played out for you to be convinced that there is no evil in you. At some point in time during the therapeutic process, there needs to be a halt to this hunt for the evil. After a considerable amount of time, I directly ask my patients whether they are convinced that no evil lies within them. Many times I simply present this concept: "You are a bright, articulate, and insightful person who has lived in your body for all these years and despite all your efforts you have found no evil. And do you know why this is?" The response from my patients always is, "Because there is not any evil there." That is exactly the point. Both you and your therapist have not found any evil because it is not there. The parasite wants you to keep hunting for the evil because this is how it maintains its grip on you. Some individuals who have come into my office have been abusers themselves. Some other patients have done terrible things to other people, sometimes to their spouses. These patients have violated the boundaries of others. They know exactly what they have done and it is at the forefront of their minds. We do not have to hunt for the evil. While I am not certain these patients are inherently evil, they certainly have done evil things and they are most aware of their evil actions.

A positive aspect of this hunt for the evil is the necessity to go back and actually give specific details of the abuse. Often, the parasite holds some details as evidence of the evil. You and your therapist need to be aware of the fact that together you need to do a detailed examination of the abuse beyond simply stating that you were abused and it was a horror. You may recall the story of Jim who was abused by his father. Jim needed to flush out some of the details of his abuse. From your standpoint, you and/or your parasite might say, "I was abused, but you do not know what I did. You do not know that I wished him dead. You do not know I prayed for the courage to stab him. You do not know I let him put his penis in my mouth." None of these things make you evil. You need to emerge from this process with the firm belief that while evil was done to you, no evil exists in you.

## VISITING THE OVENS

This section is very closely related to the previous section. My patients have demonstrated a great need to go back to the scene or scenes of their abuse. This is critical to the success of the therapeutic process. You, during your abuse, may have experienced a psychological disconnect from yourself. Many victims have reported a dissociative type of experience during the abuse/trauma, wherein a part or parts of the self seem to leave their body. They report being able to know what is happening to them, but not being able to have any feelings about what was happening. This is quite normal in any abuse/trauma situation. The immense pain of the event caused them to shut down. Perhaps an example would help. Think of the circuit breaker within an electrical panel box. If you put too much strain on a particular electrical line, the circuit breaker in the panel box trips, shutting down the power to that line. The breaker trips the line to prevent a disaster. If the breaker did not trip, the line would overheat and eventually cause an electrical fire. Clearly, the tripping of the breaker is a positive thing. In a similar fashion, defense mechanisms in humans trip in order to prevent the psychological disaster. So if you disconnected from yourself during the abuse/trauma, or have difficulty knowing what you felt, you are not alone. This is a very common occurrence in abuse/trauma situations. Given the circumstances of the trauma, your defense mechanisms tripped to protect you. Although you may feel this is problematic and at some level it is, you are still very normal and quite healthy.

What is problematic is the fact that you may need to revisit the abuse in order to reconnect with those parts of you that tripped. You may need to reconnect with your feelings that became isolated. While revisiting your abuse is certainly not pleasant and can be very painful, the revisiting of the abuse is necessary and will be most helpful to your healing.

There are other reasons why you may need to revisit the abuse/trauma. The most important reason is for you to receive validation. We have already discussed the importance of validation to your healing. What was so hurtful to April was the fact that the judge completely invalidated her abuse/trauma. As I have said so many times before, validation is essential for healing. You need someone to affirm that yes, this abuse/trauma did indeed happen. Yes, it was immensely painful. I cannot even imagine what the pain must have been like. Usually, this need for validation is not a one-time event. You may need to go back to the abuse/trauma numerous times. You and your therapist will need to continually evaluate this process.

I would like to use an analogy here. During World War II, the Holocaust occurred, wherein millions of people suffered horrible, evil atrocities. The kind of torture and suffering they experienced is incomprehensible. But those atrocities really happened. The survivors of the concentration camps needed and continued to need the people of the world to validate that this indeed did happen. They needed us to bear witness to the crimes committed against them. They needed us to commit, as a world of all nations, to never allow this to happen again. There is nothing we can do to make it up to them. There is no way we can undo what truly happened. What is done is done. No human can fix it. No human can give them back their lives.

In a similar fashion, you need this type of validation. Validation affirming that what you suffered is indeed a very personal atrocity. Validation that the violation you experienced was horrific. Validation of how incomprehensible it is that any child could be exposed to that kind of pain. Validation of the fact that we know we cannot make it better. We can only help you heal the pain that you did nothing to cause. However, while revisiting the abuse/trauma can be most helpful to the healing process, the parasite can also manipulate you into re-abusing yourself. The concern here is that when you revisit your concentration camp (your abuse/trauma), the parasite can bait you into getting back into the ovens or the gas chambers and harm yourself further. As a therapist, I have witnessed this all too often. You and your therapist must be clear on the purpose and the goal of revisiting the abuse/trauma. You will need to call forth all the parts of you to answer the following questions: What good will this revisiting of the ovens do? What do you hope to gain? What need do you hope to fulfill from this revisiting of your abuse/trauma?

At this point in my understanding of the abuse/trauma cycle and the parasite, I remain most willing to walk with my patients through the horrors of their concentration camps. However, before we go there, I freely ask them to clarify the purpose of the revisiting. I have come to routinely say to my patients, "If this will do some good, I will go to hell and back with you. However, if you are going back simply to get into the ovens or the gas chambers to reexperience or re-abuse yourself, I cannot and will not go with you. While I cannot undo the abuse/trauma you experienced, I can work at making sure I am not a part of you re-abusing yourself." When my patients hear this for the first time, they are surprised and shocked. However, after some intense discussion, they become aware of the necessity of using the yellow light concept and proceed cautiously.

# SIX

# Victim versus Survivor: Becoming a Survivor

I am sure that you have noticed that I have repeatedly used the term victim and not survivor. Perhaps this has made you quite uncomfortable. It made Lonnie uncomfortable. She wrote, "The use of the word, 'victim,' especially in the introduction was a bit shocking. The word struck me as strange and, in some sense harsh, since so much has been placed on becoming a survivor versus a victim." Jim responded quite angrily to the term victim. He wrote, "I could not believe you used the term victim throughout most of your manuscript. I found myself being quite angry. Actually John, I became really pissed off at you. You know how much I hate the term victim. I have struggled hard to become a survivor. I know what you were doing and what you hoped to accomplish. Isn't there another way?" The original outline for this text had placed this chapter last. There are several issues in this chapter that have not been addressed in detail. The original thought was that placing this chapter anywhere else in the text would only result in confusion. After receiving comments from Lonnie and Jim, as well as several other patients, it became obvious that the discussion about becoming a survivor needed to come sooner rather than later, even if it created some confusion in you, the reader. Quite honestly, I would prefer to create confusion than to cause you any discomfort. I hope I have not caused you discomfort. However, the choice of the term victim, until this point in the text, has been very purposeful. You and I both know that the parasite resulting from abuse/trauma creates a cycle of self-abuse. Here are some examples: You do things that you hope will make you feel better, only to discover that afterward you feel worse. You had a bad day at work and you are feeling lonely and disgusted. It feels like there is a war raging in your head. After last weekend and how sick you were from the amount of alcohol you consumed, you promised yourself you would not drink to ease your pain. Yet, you find yourself in the liquor cabinet. You have a drink, and you do not stop at one. You wake up the next morning feeling even more lonely and disgusted, and with how physically ill you feel as well, you wonder how you are going to make it through the day. Do you think this is self-abusive? Or perhaps, you bought a cheesecake for dessert last night for that special someone. She had to cancel; it seems that is always the way things happen to you. You are angry and you are very hurt. You have a piece of cheesecake, and the cheesecake makes you feel good. Before you know it, you have eaten half of it. The next morning you wake up, get on the scale, only to find you are up 2 more pounds, and that is 10 pounds in the past month. You go to work with this raging anger inside of you. The parasite is telling you how ugly and disgusting you are and you are listening. After work, you go to the gym and literally beat yourself up physically at the gym. Afterward, you go home and consume the other half of the cheesecake. Do you think this is self-abusive?

Another example might be as follows: You are a woman of high moral character. You have made a commitment to yourself not to have sex with just anyone because you know you only feel dirty afterward. However, you are feeling so empty and so alone; the pain is horrible. You go out with a friend for a drink and a guy asks you to dance. Afterward, you sit and talk for a while. He seems nice and is quite good looking. He thinks you are very attractive and invites you to his apartment for a drink. He wants to hold you, and before you know it is over. Wham. Bam. Thank you, Ma'am. You thought you felt pretty horrible before you went out. Now, you feel cheap, dirty, used, and disgusting. Do you think this is self-abusive? There are even worse ways of self-abuse that can end tragically.

On January 7, 2011, the *Huffington Post* reported, "Bill Zeller, a Princeton PhD candidate and a renowned Internet programmer died Wednesday from injuries sustained in a suicide attempt. He was 27. Zeller stunned the programming community with a 4000 word suicide note detailing a history of childhood physical and sexual abuse, which he had never disclosed to anyone." Mr. Zeller's suicide note is graphic and quite disturbing. He details, what for him, became insurmountable pain and the reasons he chose to take his own life. You may be wondering why I would even mention such a disturbing note in this book, which needs to be filled with hope about recovering from abuse/trauma. It is included in this text in order to assist you in choosing to become a survivor. Tragically, Mr. Zeller succumbed to the parasite that he called the darkness. In this situation, the parasite consumed the host and possibly has replicated itself in those who knew and loved Mr. Zeller. Many of my patients have contemplated suicide as a means of ending their pain. Thankfully they have chosen life over death. They have chosen to become survivors and not remain victims.

You may not be involved in the depths of self-abusive behaviors that I have described earlier. However, you need to be honest with yourself and remember it is critical that you do not minimize the toll your abuse/trauma has taken on you. Many times victims victimize themselves inside their heads. They allow the parasite to engage in self-depreciating litanies. These litanies include self-repudiation, self-punishment, self-hate, and self-debasement, just to name a few. There is nothing trivial about the pain these litanies create in a victim. If you are engaging in any or all of the litanies described previously, you are allowing yourself to remain a victim. You are allowing the parasite to continually re-create the pain of the abuse/trauma you experienced.

You are probably asking the following question: "So how do I become a survivor?" You need to embrace the fact that becoming a survivor is a process, not an event. It is a process that you need to take one day at a time, one step at a time. Becoming a survivor requires you to make healthier choices in your life. Today, you did not drink. Today, you did not eat the cheesecake. Today, you did not allow someone to take sexual advantage of you. Today, you chose to take the power back from the parasite. Today, you chose life over death. You may have wanted to, or even felt the need to, engage in your negative habituated behaviors. Acknowledge this reality and never lie to yourself. You need to feel empowered by the fact that, while you felt the desire to engage in self-destructive behaviors, you chose healing. This begins the cycle of becoming a survivor. This cycle will take time and much energy, but you can and will become a survivor. It is your choice.

There are several stages you need to experience in this process of becoming a survivor. Notice Dr. Ross and I used the term stages and not steps. You will find that there is an ebb and flow to the process of becoming a survivor. The parasite will use this ebb and flow to frustrate and depress you. It will also use fear to thwart your efforts in becoming a survivor. You may find the parasite saying, "Remember the higher up you are, the harder you fall." This is another aspect where you need to use the yellow light concept and proceed cautiously. Regardless of what the parasite tells you, you need to keep your eye on the goal of surviving and being a survivor. When I was completing my doctoral studies, it began to feel as if I was climbing a mountain that someone or something kept making higher and higher. Sometimes when you are on a journey, you need to look back and see how far you have come in the journey. In essence, you need to keep one eye on the goal and one eye on how many miles you have already traversed in your journey. In doing this, you will be able to constantly be aware of the goal, and this will help you to keep focused. Keeping one eye on the progress you have made simultaneously will enable you to be encouraged by the work that you have accomplished. The stages of recovery are detailed later. Stages 1 and 2 need to be taken in order. The next several stages need to be taken as you see fit and, hopefully, with the guidance of your therapist. Some stages will be more important to you than others, and it is important that you use these stages as individually necessary. Stages were not designed as a one-size-fits-all methodology. Rather, the stages are established as guideposts for you in order to examine what you believe you need to do to heal. You may come to establish other stages that I have not listed. Trust in yourself and the magic that exists in you. The following are the 14 stages that comprise the process of becoming a true survivor.

Stage 1: Admitting that you have experienced abuse/trauma and have someone validate this reality and the feelings that accompany it. You may have attempted to do this before, perhaps with a family member, a good friend, or even a professional. It may have turned into a disaster wherein the person you trusted with your secret, minimized your abuse, tried to fix it, or worst of all did not believe you. If this is the case, I am truly sorry. You need to do it again, this time with a professional you have confidence in and can trust completely. Bill Zeller cited several reasons why he felt he could not trust a professional (Zeller, 2011). He never recognized that all these reasons were little more than parasitic mantras. Do not allow your parasite to prevent you from getting the help you need. Once your abuse/trauma has been validated, you need to begin to integrate that validation and own it for yourself.

Stage 2: Begin to accept that this indeed is a part of you, a part of you that you cannot change. However, keep in mind, that it is just that, a part of you, not *all* of you. Recognizing that the abuse/trauma is just a part of you is essential to you becoming a survivor because you have a sense of a today and a tomorrow that is not dictated by yesterday. Since I have already discussed acceptance in great detail, I will not repeat it here. Again, stages 1 and 2 need to be taken in order.

Stage 3: You need to take an honest account of the strengths you have as a person. I know you do not feel you have any, but you already know that is impossible, so please get to work on this positive inventory. Take a piece of paper and write down those good and positive qualities. Take the paper and put it on the refrigerator or your bedroom mirror, and constantly think about those good qualities. Your thinking about these qualities will eventually enable you to feel those good qualities inside of you. Use the evidence found in your daily life to both support and reinforce the reality that these positive qualities *do* exist in you. You need to work at accepting compliments and not allow the parasite to refute them and just blow the compliments off. This positive account will be of great importance to you in order to accomplish stage 4.

Stage 4: You now need to begin to work at altering your perception of yourself. This stage has been detailed in chapter 4.

Stage 5: Work at splitting the emotions of sadness, guilt, and shame. This will enable you to begin to decrease responsibility that you carry for the abuse/trauma.

Stage 6: Grieve what has been lost, a part or all of your childhood and/or adolescence. You may need, like Lonnie, to grieve the loss of a true parent that you never had.

Stage 7: Recognize that there is a spiritual dimension to your person-hood. It would be most helpful to you if you could come to terms with the Spirit. The Spirit will help you perceive a goodness that exists outside of you as simply a reflection of the goodness that exists within you.

Stage 8: Recognize that regardless of the circumstances of your abuse/trauma, you are not responsible for the abuse/trauma. The only responsibility that is yours is the responsibility to heal yourself because no one else can heal you. You did not ask for the abuse/trauma, and you are not at fault. It is completely unfair and unjust that you are in a position where you need to work so hard at healing. Nonetheless, it is the only way to becoming a true survivor.

Stage 9: Embrace the reality that you are human, and while you may despise your frailties, you cannot change the fact that you are human. This will enable you to establish appropriate boundaries for yourself, your drive for perfection, and your desire to people please. Boundaries, perfectionism, and people-pleasing will be discussed in the next few chapters.

Stage 10: Come to fully believe and embrace the fact that your abuse/trauma has resulted in ego fragmentation. You are not damaged, regardless of what the parasite tells you. Regrettably, Bill Zeller never accepted this as his reality. His darkness or his parasite told him he was broken and damaged and that was the reality he accepted. If only he could have found some hope in his ability to recover, perhaps he could have embraced the belief that his ego was simply fragmented, not broken or damaged. I will discuss the significant difference between fragmented and damaged in chapter 10.

Stage 11: Reestablish trust in the self and in others. Your trust has been violated and this has resulted in you having difficulty trusting others as well as significant difficulty trusting yourself. The parasite has played on your emotions as well as your sense of responsibility for the abuse/trauma, which has resulted in your distrust of self. There will be more detail on reestablishing trust in yourself and others in a subsequent chapter.

Stage 12: Learn to forgive yourself. Since I have been telling you throughout this text that you are not responsible for the abuse/trauma, you may be wondering why I would be discussing your need to learn about forgiving yourself. This is exactly the confusion I was concerned about in placing this chapter before the end of the text. I would ask you to simply think about how I have constructed the difference between survivor and victim. If you have been involved in significant self-abusive behaviors, you will need to learn to forgive yourself for those transgressions. This will be detailed in the next chapter.

Stage 13: Establish appropriate and pliable boundaries for your person-hood. The boundary violation of abuse/trauma has resulted in your difficulty to establish appropriate boundaries for yourself and for others. If you are like many of my patients, you find yourself keeping everyone at a significant emotional distance from you, or more equally problematic, allowing everyone to take advantage of you. Boundaries are crucial to healthy emotional functioning, and you need to learn to establish appropriate boundaries that have necessary and sufficient pliability. This will be detailed in chapter 9.

Stage 14: Establish appropriate boundaries for your people-pleasing and perfectionism tendencies. The parasite has convinced you that your abuse/trauma has resulted in you being less than those other people around you. In order to compensate for you being less than, you attempted to please people at any cost. You have driven yourself to strive for perfection knowing it cannot be attained and yet believing this was the only way you could make up for all the personal deficits your abuse/trauma created. We will be discussing these concepts in great detail in chapter 10.

Using these 14 stages, you need to make a firm commitment to work at curtailing and eventually stopping the self-abusive cycle. I encourage you to begin to treat yourself with the respect and trust you need. I hope you had an opportunity to see the movie *What about Bob?* If you have not seen this, I would encourage you to do so. It is funny and filled with paradoxes.

The psychiatrist in the movie wrote a book entitled *Baby Steps*. Psychology has, for a long time, used the phrase "Incremental Goal Attainment Scaling" or (as in the movie) the simpler phrase "baby steps." Employing the concept of baby steps is exactly how I would encourage you to approach your journey to becoming a true survivor. It is important that you go slowly and cautiously into this new territory. Take pride in your successes no matter how small they may seem to you. The parasite will bate you into minimizing any of your successes. Do not take the bait. Your success will give you power and actually diminish the parasite's power. You need this power to keep on your journey of becoming a survivor.

One of my mentors, Guido D. Boriosi, MD, is a psychiatrist with whom I credit my success in private practice. Dr. Boriosi (2002) wrote a book entitled *Understanding Yourself: It's So Darn Easy*. In his book, Dr. Boriosi discusses the four P's to becoming healthier:

(1) Prayer

(2) Pills

(3) Patience

(4) Push (p. 121)

I would like to have another P for Persistence and also change the order. So my five P's are:

(1) Prayer

(2) Patience

(3) Push

(4) Persistence

(5) Pills

(1) Prayer: Dr. Boriosi reports that this is self-explanatory, and while I agree with him, it is important to note just how important some kind of connection or communion with the Spirit truly is. Both patients and students have asked me whether I believe healing can occur without some connection with a spiritual dimension. Honestly, I am really not sure. However, I am very sure that the journey to become a survivor is, indeed, more difficult without a connection to one's spirituality and a Spirit.

(2) Patience: Genuine healing is a very slow process. Similar to physical healing from surgery or a debilitating illness, psychological healing can

seem like it takes forever. There are no quick fixes. No matter how well you my might progress, it will never be quick enough for you because you are in pain. You need to be patient. In order to be very clear about the term patience, it may be best to define patience. The *APA Dictionary* does not define patience, but *Webster's Dictionary* has several different definitions for this term. The one that is most appropriate is, "3. quiet, steady, perseverance; even-tempered care; diligence." This definition is a great fit to what I have been telling you. Do you remember the fable of the tortoise and the hare? Keep in mind that the steady pace you set for yourself will get you across the finish line.

(3) Push: Pain whether it is physical, psychological, or spiritual is extremely energy depleting. Your fatigue is most real. You have been struggling with the parasite and that has taken an incredible amount of energy. You will need to push yourself to do things even when you do not feel you have the energy. From time to time, you may get a burst of energy. We tend to overdo when we feel this burst of energy. Enjoy the good feeling, but be very cautious about not overdoing. A slow, even steady pace produces the best results in healing.

(4) Persistence: When you commit to working at a goal, you may not always be completely successful, but you are working at it, and that will give you energy. *Webster's Dictionary* defines persistence as "the act or fact of persisting" and defines the verb persist as "to continue steadily or firmly in some state, purpose, or course of action, in spite of opposition or criticism." The parasite will, from time to time, strongly oppose you and provide you with much criticism. Persist in the baby steps, because that is exactly what the parasite does not want.

(5) Pills: The trauma of abuse is often associated with anxiety and mood disorders. At times you may feel both anxious and depressed. Your therapist may have recommended you see a medical doctor for possible medication to help stabilize your neurochemistry and to reduce some of the symptoms you are experiencing. Your therapist may not be a medical doctor, yet therapists do know that medication can aid our patients in recovering. Psychotropic medications are slow acting and they will not just heal you without much hard work on your part. There are no happy pills, but medication can be a crucial aspect to your recovering.

I would like to give you a very personal example of how I used the five P's. When I began writing this book, it felt like someone had given me a spoon and placed me on a beach on the New Jersey coast and said, "Get all the sand off of this beach." My parasite kept saying things like, "You will never pull this off. This time, pal, you have really bitten off more than you can chew. Who the hell do you think you are anyway?" Writing this text, similar to your healing, was a very slow process. Understand that I am not equating the task of writing a book to the task you have ahead of you. Rather I am asking you to look at the process. I did a fair amount of praying, asking the Spirit for help and guidance. There were days that I sat at the computer and did not get one word typed. My parasite was depleting my energy and telling me to just give it up. There were days when my eyes hurt from how tired I became. However, I kept working at it and persisted in my goal.

Again, the task of writing a book is nowhere near the difficult challenge before you. Becoming a survivor is not easy and it does not just happen. I trust that you are feeling a sense of hope as well as a sense of empowerment. Take that first step and begin walking the walk. Begin the journey of becoming-becoming a true survivor. Perhaps, it would be important to you to examine how some of my patients, those you have met and those you have not, became survivors.

## SADIE

Sadie is a 36-year-old African American married female. She has been married for seven years and has two female children from this union: Jackie age seven and Christy age four. Her biological father is deceased, having died in 1999 at the age of 50 and her biological mother is 62 and in good health. Mother resides in the Midwest. Sadie was an only child. Her parents divorced at Sadie's age seven, and she had little to no contact with the father after the divorce.

Sadie reported moving to Northeastern Pennsylvania about nine months ago. Her husband is a government employee who was transferred to this area. The family currently resides in a residential community that she describes as a predominately white unfriendly community. She is and was a stay-at-home mom since the birth of Jackie. She reported feelings of sadness, bouts of tearfulness, disruptions in sleep, cognitions, appetite, and short-term memory. These symptoms have been present for the past year, but have significantly increased during the past several months. She went to her primary care physician at the begging of her husband. Her primary care physician medically cleared her and referred her to me. Homicidal ideations were denied, but she admitted to suicidal ideations, which she stated have intensified the past six weeks. She stated that she has become terrified because "I started thinking about ways to do it," which include pills and autocide.

Sadie reported that her father was a professional in Georgia. She describes him as a raging functional alcoholic who was physically and emotionally abusive to her mom. She denied physical abuse from the father but admitted to emotional abuse. She said that when she was six, "My mom got me a puppy." The puppy apparently chewed one of her father's shoes. He was very drunk and took the dog out into the yard and stabbed it to death and said to Sadie, "Let that be a lesson, child." Sadie's mom divorced her dad and moved to the Midwest where her mom had extended family.

She remembers this event like it was yesterday. She has recurring nightmares about dogs. She stated when she encounters dogs, she falls apart, which includes crying hysterical, feelings of horror, and helplessness. She reports rage toward her father and self-hatred and guilt for not saving her puppy. Her children have begged her for a puppy and she vehemently refuses. She avoids taking her children to parks, and so forth, where dogs might be. She moved to a no-pet condo in this area.

She reports being estranged from her mother since age 15, when Sadie became sexually active. She reports that she went from boyfriend to boyfriend and never felt love, and dumped them before they could dump her. She met her present husband in graduate school and reports he is very devoted to her. However, lately he has become quite angry with her behavior. She admits never being faithful in the marriage. She stated that she is not sure why she cheats on him, but really cannot stop herself. She reports that being a stay-at-home mom allows her to act out, and she is happy with this arrangement.

She reported being an A student in high school, but she kept to herself. She completed a BA in elementary education with a B average. There were no extracurricular activities in college. She did work for several years as a teacher, but was let go from four different schools because "I was too strict."

She reported being in treatment, on and off, since the age of 15. She stated that it did not help at all. She reported either discontinuing treatment on her own or being discharged because "they (therapists) did not like her." She attempted suicide at age 19, after being dumped by a manipulative older man who used her like her father. (She denied any sexual abuse by her father.)

Sadie admitted to experimenting in high school with numerous drugs, but her drug of choice is currently vodka. She admits to daily use, and drinking and driving. She denied ever risking driving under the influence with her children in the car.

Sadie reported having a friend in the Midwest with whom she would act out. "She was just like me." She keeps in touch by e-mail and phone, and she misses the fun she had with her. She has made no friends since moving to this area.

During her next few sessions, I explored the issues of her emotional abuse. Sadie began to tell her tale of horrible abuse by her father. He would call her names that are not fit to print and would tell her how worthless she was. He blamed her for his drinking, because he wished she was never born. Sadie detested her father but also blamed her mother for not protecting her from this beast.

I began to introduce the aspect of how this abuse had affected her, and she genuinely felt some relief with the concept of the parasite. As she began to trust me, Sadie also began to confide that she was very concerned about her drinking. She was concerned about the quantity and the fact that she was getting more and more risky regarding her drinking and driving, and was concerned that she might place her children in harm's way.

I told Sadie that the first problem we needed to address was her drinking and her drinking and driving. I suggested that she see a drug and alcohol specialist and begin attending Alcoholics Anonymous (AA) meetings. With this, Sadie became furious and stormed out of the office. I did not see her again for about six months.

When I next saw Sadie, she had been arrested for a DUI. She was remorseful and completely humiliated because the children were in the car. I asked Sadie whether she was now ready to do battle with the parasite. She told me that she was sick of feeling worthless and helpless. She admitted that she had been having suicidal ideations, but believed that her children needed their mother to not just "punch out on them." She also told me, "My husband is at the end of his rope with me." I offered to see Sadie and her husband together, and they agreed. When I discussed the parasite model with the couple, the husband told me he felt relieved because he was finally able to appreciate what was happening to his wife and his life. I explained that because of ethical issues, I was not able to do marital therapy with the couple, but I could refer them to colleagues. They agreed. Sadie agreed to work also with an alcohol specialist and allowed me to coordinate her care with the alcohol specialist.

While the parasite model made a great deal of sense to Sadie on a cognitive (thought) level, she had significant difficulty with the model on an affective (emotional) level. She, like so many others, resisted admitting that she was a victim of abuse. The parasite kept baiting her to somehow erase what happened to her in childhood and the devastating impact it was having on her adulthood. The parasite also manipulated her with the notion that she was a psychologically weak individual and that she somehow just needed to get over this. She needed to admit that she was abused and that this abuse was traumatic. She also needed to accept that she suffered from a posttraumatic stress disorder. The symptoms that she reported to me were classic in regard to a posttraumatic stress disorder. What she failed to realize is that the alcohol and the acting out sexually were nothing more than her futile attempts to self-medicate her symptomatology.

You may be asking, "What is a posttraumatic stress disorder?" Posttraumatic stress disorder is a diagnosis that typically reflects many of the symptoms of abuse/trauma. The *APA Dictionary of Psychology* defines posttraumatic stress disorder as "a disorder that results when an individual lives through or witnesses an event in which he or she believes that there is a threat to life or physical integrity and safety and experiences fear, terror, or helplessness. The symptoms are characterized by (a) reexperiencing of the trauma in painful recollections, flashbacks, or current dreams and nightmares; (b) diminished responsiveness (emotional anesthesia or numbing), with disinterest in significant activities and feelings of detachment and estrangement from others; and (c) chronic physiological arousal, leading to such symptoms as exaggerated startle response, disturbed sleep, difficulty in concentrating or remembering, guilt about surviving what others did not, and avoidance of activities that call the traumatic event to mind."

Recall that abuse/trauma can be acute or chronic. In Sadie's case, it was both. The verbal thrashings that Sadie received from her father most of her childhood certainly constitute chronic abuse/trauma. The stabbing of her puppy and being told that this was to teach her a lesson would constitute acute abuse/trauma. I would ask you not to get caught up in the diagnosis because it is placed here simply to help you understand Sadie's circumstances. It is also hoped that, by using the diagnosis, it might provide you with some of the feelings you may be experiencing. Work at remembering that the parasite will use anything and everything to distract you from understanding what happened to you and then using that understanding to heal.

After a significant length of time, Sadie finally surrendered to the reality of the pain she experienced at the hands of her father and the total sense of abandonment from her mother. Once Sadie began to deflect the parasite's minimization of her pain, she began to truly validate her pain on an emotional level. However, once she was able to accomplish this, the parasite opened floodgates of her anger toward both of her parents. The anger terrified her. She knew on a thought level that she was angry, but never really allowed herself to feel this anger. I asked her to keep in mind that the anger she was now experiencing was always there, and the parasite manipulated her into taking this anger out on herself. As she began to both accept and embrace the terror that she felt regarding her feelings, she was able to begin to truly see the cycle of her self abuse. The parasite was able to use the anger she had turned inward to enable her sexual acting out. The resulting guilt she felt regarding her sexual acting out only served to exacerbate her pain. The parasite then took this pain and baited her into self-medicating with alcohol. The parasite kept the cycle going until she felt completely out-of-control. The sexual acting out and the drinking that were supposed to alleviate her pain only served to enmesh her in her pain.

What was at the core of Sadie's difficulties was her belief that she was damaged and broken as evidence to her by her own parents not being able to love her because she was, in fact, unlovable. Her sexual acting out was a parasitic solution to her feelings of being unlovable. However, the more she acted out sexually, the more she felt unlovable and damaged. Sadie was engaged in a dramatic negative self-fulfilling prophecy. Her perception that she was damaged energized the parasite, and the parasite used the words deserving and worthy against her. Sadie had verbalized that she felt damaged by her abuse/trauma. However, I was unaware of how the parasite used this perception of being damaged against her. After nine months of intense therapy, Sadie began to reveal how much she truly loved her husband. Sadie and I then began to work on answering the following question: "If I love him that much, what would make me behave in a manner to drive him away by hurting him so much with these affairs?" Sadie became very reticent in response to this question. Sadie stated, "I must be broken and damaged. That certainly explains why my father and mother found me unlovable. If my own parents found me unlovable, that proves that I am unlovable. It is just a matter of time before he becomes sick of me and my behaviors and abandons me, just like my mother neglected me emotionally. If I was not worthy or deserving of my parents' love as a child, certainly this adult woman is completely unworthy and undeserving of this wonderful man's love."

It is important that you and I closely examine what Sadie revealed and sort out the workings of the parasite in Sadie. Developmentally, as a child, Sadie attempted to make sense out of her abuse and neglect. The only reasonable explanation she, as a child, could ascertain was that she was damaged and broken. Sadie attempted to make sense where no sense could be made. But the parasite helped her make sense in her no-sense world.

Establishing the perception that she was broken and damaged not only provided Sadie with the sense of order in her world, but also provided her with the sense of responsibility for the abuse by the father and the mother's neglect. Can you recognize Sadie's erroneous thinking? Can you recognize your own erroneous thinking?

One of the first major breakthroughs for Sadie was the realization that she had several choices to make at this point in her life. She could choose to remain victim. She could choose to continue drinking. She could choose to continue to act out sexually. She could choose to lose her children and her husband. She could, like Bill Zeller, choose death over life. Initially Sadie really did not view these as choices. The parasite initially would not allow her to feel empowered by making healthy choices. When she came to realize that no one could force her to do anything to alter her life, she became empowered with the reality that she could truly choose a different course. With the admission that she had been victimized by her father and mother, and her choice to accept what had happened as unchangeable, Sadie began to integrate the validation of her pain. With this validation, Sadie chose to become a survivor. She chose to stop drinking and began attending AA meetings. She chose to stop the acting-out behaviors and she chose to rebuild her family. She chose life over death.

During the course of her treatment, Sadie began to use several of the stages outlined in this chapter. One of the key stages for Sadie was the splitting of the emotions of sadness, guilt, and shame. This led to a significant decrease in the responsibility that she carried for her abuse/trauma. She began to grieve her childhood and the parents she truly never had. At some point in her grieving process, the parasite began to bait her into the hunt for the evil and the visiting the ovens games simultaneously. Thankfully, Sadie was able to uncover a major stumbling block for her healing. Sadie had never mentioned the fact that her father was a minister in a fundamental Christian church. Needless to say that Sadie had a major issue with the Spirit, and she was having great difficulty in recognizing a goodness that existed in her. After a great deal of discussion regarding the impact of the father being a minister in a fairly dogmatic church, it became obvious that, through her sexual acting out, Sadie was lashing out at her father, mother, and the Spirit. "How could a man who professed to believe in a Spirit say and do those awful things to his own child? How could a woman who professed to believe in the Spirit allow a man to do those awful things and do nothing to protect her child? How could a Spirit who was supposedly all good and loving allow innocent children to suffer such inhumanity?" Notice, Sadie used the phrase "innocent children." This was an incredible step forward in Sadie's healing process. Having used the phrase "innocent children," Sadie was now in touch with the healthy parts of her ego. While she could not find the goodness that existed in her at this particular time, she was able to see the goodness that existed in her husband and her children. Reluctantly, she began to come to terms with the Spirit. Once she began to separate the Spirit from her mother and father, and she began to see the Spirit in her husband and children, she was actually able to begin to recognize some of her own goodness. With this, she was able to initiate altering the perception of herself. There were several other stages that Sadie worked through during her recovery process. You and I will visit those stages in subsequent chapters of this text. For now, we will leave Sadie, but before we do, I want to share with you that Sadie has recently celebrated five years of sobriety. She has ceased all sexual acting-out behaviors and has rebuilt her marriage and family.

## JOSEPHINE

At the time Josephine and I first began working together, she was a 66-year-old Caucasian married woman. She had been married for 45 years and had two adult female children, aged 42 and 39, as a result of this union. Her older daughter was married and had two female children, aged 8 and 6. Both of Josephine's parents were deceased, and she had one younger brother, aged 61, with whom she had a very distant relationship. She indicated that she had a very close marital relationship and that she was "eternally grateful to my husband for putting up with all my crap."

Josephine reported that she had been battling a panic disorder for most of her life. Over the course of many years, she had been treated by several different psychiatrists who "gave me the pills and told me I had nothing to fear." Seven years ago, after the birth of her first granddaughter, Josephine began seeing a therapist who worked out of the hospital where she was employed as a secretary. Josephine stated that she was very committed to not allowing her panic disorder to destroy the time she might have with her grandchildren. She indicated that the therapy she had received had helped to some degree, but the therapist closed his practice and she was forced to seek another therapist.

Josephine was more than reluctant to discuss her developmental history, other than to state that her parents were poor immigrants and that her father was a wonderful, hardworking man. Her mother was a stay-at-home mom, who as reported by Josephine had a terrible problem with her emotions. Her mother reportedly spent several years in various psychiatric institutions. Her father did what he could to fill in the gaps with her mom being hospitalized, but relied heavily on Josephine to be the mom of the house when she was nine years old, providing total care for her 5-year-old brother. When she was 10 years old, Josephine's mother was discharged from the psychiatric institution, but Josephine was required to stay home from school because "mom was too afraid to be alone." Josephine reluctantly admitted that she longed for a mother who would take care of her and shower her with hugs and kisses, but that never happened. Instead, Josephine was required to be the mother of the house and to be a mother to her mother. In addition, Josephine, over time, described her mother as a woman, who besides being filled with fears, was self-centered, selfish, demanding, and oblivious to the needs of her children and her husband. She indicated that her father was a good man but was totally devoted to her mother and never willing to be the father she needed him to be. When she was 13 years old and struggling desperately to keep up with her academics, she was befriended by a middle-aged male teacher. "He told me that he saw something special in me and was willing to stay after school to help me catch up on my studies. In the beginning, he was very kind, gentle, and funny. After a while, he started giving me hugs when I would leave his classroom. I really wanted my father to hug me, but he was too busy. These hugs from the teacher made me feel strange, but I kept staying after school and enjoying his company. He was really helping me with my academics. One day he took me into the closet of the classroom. He asked me if I really liked him and I said yes. Then he pulled down his pants and asked me to show him how much I liked him." Josephine stated that I was the first person she had ever talked to about her real childhood history, not even telling her husband what happened to her. The anger and the pain that I sensed in Josephine was overwhelming. In addition to the anger and the pain, she was terrified that I would think less of her. I certainly reassured her that this was not the case, and I began the process of validating what had happened to her and her right to the subsequent feelings her pain created.

It is important that you know that all of this information did not surface during the first session, or even the first several sessions. It took almost a year before this information was shared. I have seen incredible fear in people, but I do not think I ever witnessed the kind of terror I saw on Josephine's face when she reported this information. The parasite had such a stranglehold on her that she truly believed that if she told anyone, that person would confirm just how dirty, disgusting, and evil she was. Of course,

I told her that I did not see her as dirty, disgusting, or evil, and of course, she did not believe me. It took her several months before she was able to really integrate that she was not dirty, disgusting, or evil. She crumbled in the chair and began sobbing and said, "I feel so lost." I responded, "Josie, if you are ever going to find yourself, you need to first admit you are lost. This is a real turning point for you." And it, indeed, was the turning point for Josephine. How this woman was able to bear this insurmountable pain for 53 years is quite honestly beyond me. What is not beyond me though is the incredible, magical resilience this woman displayed in coping with both her pain and her panic disorder with agoraphobia.

As with the ethical caution presented in the case of Sadie, it is perhaps important that we define the diagnosis of panic disorder with agoraphobia. However, it is even more important that we do not get caught up in the diagnosis and that we never attempt to diagnose ourselves. This is something I say repeatedly when I am teaching the Dysfunction and Pathology Course in our program. Symptoms can often be so vague that we could probably fit ourselves at some level into every diagnostic category in the diagnostic manual. This diagnostic information is included simply to help you understand how abuse can and does manifest itself in so many different ways. I implore you, please do not self-diagnose. In order to give you accurate information, agoraphobia and panic disorder are defined separately. The *APA Dictionary of Psychology* defines agoraphobia as "literally fear of the marketplace from the (Greek word agora) manifested as anxiety about being in places or situations for fear of having uncontrolled panic symptoms or panic attacks. Apprehension is typically focused on the fear of being unable to avoid a situation from which escape may be difficult or to control the panic symptoms that may result from exposure to the situation. The types of situations that are avoided (or endured with significant distress) include standing in line, being in a crowd, and traveling in a bus or train or car. Agoraphobia may accompany a panic disorder (panic disorder with agoraphobia) in which an individual experiences unexpected panic attacks."

Panic disorder is defined by the *APA Dictionary of Psychology* as "an anxiety disorder characterized by our current, unexpected panic attacks that are associated with (a) persistent concern about having another attack, (b) worry about the possible consequences of the attacks, (c) significant change in behavior related to attacks (e.g., avoiding situations, engaging in safety behavior, not going out alone), (d) a combination of any or all of these. Panic disorder associated with significant avoidance is classified as panic disorder with agoraphobia."

Josephine's parasite had her so completely enmeshed in her panic disorder that she spent the majority of her life attempting to control the symptoms, thereby never getting to the cause of the symptoms.

Josephine's parasite really played the hunt for the evil game exceptionally well. Josephine had reported to me that because of her panic disorder, she was unable to attend very important milestones in the lives of her children. Events that you and I might simply take for granted, such as school graduations, presented Josephine with absolutely intolerable situations. Her husband and children verbally acknowledged an understanding of why mom cannot be there, but this only fed the parasite with more and more guilt. It also established that Josephine was something less than most other people. Josephine informed me that several years ago when her daughter was being married, Josephine, because of her fear of dying or going crazy during a panic attack, hired an ambulance with paramedics to park behind the church and the reception hall just in case she needed them. After she related this incredible story, she stated, "Now tell me how crazy that is, and tell me how disgusting you really think I am." I recall vividly just sitting there for a few minutes and thinking to myself that I would never in a million years have thought of something so brilliant and so resilient. I told Josephine just what I thought. Instead of the parasite actually shocking me, the tables were turned and she was in utter shock. Josephine later stated that she believed that moment was a significant turning point in her beginning to alter her perception of the self.

Stage 5 of the recovery process presented Josephine with a major stumbling block. Her parasite had her caught between tremendous guilt and complete shame, and this is how the parasite kept her bearing all the responsibility for her abuse/trauma. Josephine's parasite had convinced her that she encouraged the sexual abuse from the teacher. A breakthrough came on this issue when I started to place her granddaughters in the position Josephine was in during her childhood. Josephine became quite agitated and angry that I would even conceive of her granddaughters being in that horrible situation. Josephine was encouraged to use that anger and agitation against the parasite, and by using baby steps she was able to relinquish some of the responsibility for her abuse/trauma. However, she also carried an enormous sense of guilt and responsibility due to the fact that she felt she had failed as a mother because she succumbed to her panic disorder and deprived her husband and children of so many things. This was indeed the reality. Yes, Josephine was not in attendance at many of the family events. However, the reality was and is that Josephine was an incredibly wonderful mother who was there to provide the love, the hugs, the guidance, and the support that Josephine's mother was unable to provide for Josephine and her brother. Josephine's positively altered perception, wherein she saw herself as being resilient, provided her with enough stamina to ward off the parasite to begin to gradually decrease her sense of responsibility for the panic disorder and the subsequent difficulties it created. She was able to connect with the reality that the panic disorder was ultimately a result of the neglect and sexual abuse/trauma she experienced.

Josephine resided three blocks away from a hospital. Twenty years ago she applied for a job as a secretary at the hospital. She eventually worked her way into becoming the ward clerk for the emergency room. She noted that once she became the ward clerk for the emergency room, she began to feel a sense of safety for the first time in her life. She felt safer at work than any other place, including home. To this day, she remains employed in this position. However, she has expanded her safety zone to now include her home and her daughters' homes. If one knows anything about panic disorder with agoraphobia and the ultimate fear of dying or going crazy, then one would realize that this is the ultimate job for a person suffering from a panic disorder with agoraphobia. This is yet another demonstration of incredible resilience found in Josephine. The fact that Josephine hired an ambulance to park in the back of the church and the reception hall and the fact that she procured a job in an emergency room are together key indicators that Josephine started becoming the survivor long before she met me or her previous therapist. Josephine's parasite twisted both of these indicators of her resilience in her mind to be nothing more than an indicator of her insanity and her weakness. Josephine chose to alter her perception of these issues and to embrace them as indicators of her resilience. This action resulted in Josephine altering her perception of herself. The better she felt about herself, the stronger she became in her struggle against the parasite. Josephine's struggle with the parasite also demonstrated a very important point regarding the 14 stages. As you and I have discussed, the first two stages need to be taken in order, while the other stages need to be addressed as you see fit. For Josephine, the third stage served as a significant source of strength and stamina regarding her working at the other stages. When she attempted to address stages 4 and 5, Josephine found herself hitting a brick wall. She was encouraged to bypass these stages and simply move on to a stage she felt would provide her with additional strength and stamina. Stage 6 became that additional source of strength and stamina. She already had a remarkably positive image of the Spirit. She was encouraged to use her positive relationship with the Spirit in her struggle with the parasite. There were many times when she said to me,

"I feel as if there is an angry little girl running around inside of me, and I really do not know what to do with her." I would ask her if she thought her Spirit might know what to do with this child. With an affirmative response, I would then encourage her to imagine placing this child in the arms of her Spirit. Using her positive relationship with her Spirit became routine for Josephine and allowed her to incorporate her own sense of goodness. We will examine her continued struggle with some of the stages of her journey of recovery. It is important for you to know that Josephine has accomplished some remarkable goals in her struggle with the parasite, including vacationing with their grandchildren.

## JIM

It is perhaps very important to examine the difficulty some individuals have with stages 1 and 2, the admission of what has happened and the acceptance of the unchangeableness of what has happened. The reality is that in order to find yourself you must first admit you are lost. You may recall the story of Jim we discussed in chapter 2. Jim was the young man whose father had inflicted severe physical and emotional abuse on Jim and his brothers. The father would go to the extremes of chasing Jim and his brothers around the house with a loaded weapon. Jim's parasite would actually use some of the father's statements to prevent Jim from admitting and accepting his abuse. Jim heard his father make statements over and over, such as, "Be a man, you pieces of shits. Suck it up. Quit you baby whimpering." The statements became so ingrained in Jim's psyche that the parasite was able to use the statements to inhibit Jim from admitting and accepting what pain he had endured at his father's hands. Jim was very reluctant to discuss his abuse in any detail, and he would purposely avoid any expression of feeling. When Jim finally began to discuss the abuse with me, he would become quite emotional. After the session, Jim's parasite would begin raging and, using the father statements, would produce evidence that Jim's father was actually right. The parasite would convince him he was not a man at all. He was a whimpering baby. The major difficulty here was not so much with what the parasite was doing, but rather the fact that Jim would not tell me what was happening. Here the parasite used the emotion of shame to inhibit Jim's recovery. Jim was simply too ashamed to tell me what was happening to him. I knew there was some difficulty, but unfortunately I have not been blessed with the ability to read minds. Let Jim's struggle be a lesson to all of us that you really need to be able to report as much as possible to your therapist.

When Jim finally opened up and told me what was happening, together we were able to create buffers for Jim to use against the parasite. Jim was able to embrace the fact that these statements, made by his father, and now used by the parasite as parasitic mantras, were simply nothing more than that, parasitic mantras. Jim was able to see the insanity in these parasitic mantras and actually begin to use his own humor to ward off these mantras. When the parasite would start its chatter in his head, Jim would simply repeat over and over again, "My parasite is as crazy as my old man." After a short period of time, Jim began to experience a considerable degree of success against his parasite and was finally able to begin the process involved in stages 1 and 2. However, Jim would be the first to tell you that things got worse before they got better. I am using this example to reinforce the fact that sometimes, particularly at the beginning of your recovery, things might seem worse to you. The reality is they are. The parasite will in essence use all its energy to keep you from engaging in the process of recovering. The most important issue for you is to recognize what is happening, share it with your therapist, and do everything possible not to allow your discouragement to keep you a victim. You have the ability and the stamina, and you have chosen to be a survivor. Hold on to that. If you need an additional source of strength and courage, I ask you to turn to the Spirit. I have seen many parasites. They are all cunning, shrewd, and baffling. Parasites are highly resistive to treatment because of their strength. But I have never encountered a parasite that is stronger than the person and the person's Spirit.

Again, many of my students and most of my patients have asked me directly whether I believe an individual can recover from the pain and suffering created by abuse/trauma without a sense of the Spirit. Because I have been privileged to witness the amazing resilience within so many incredible people, I would be remiss if I did not say yes. Yet, while I affirm that people have this incredible resilience, I also believe that it is the grace of the Spirit that gives them this resilience. I hold firmly that while individuals might be able to recover fully from their abuse/trauma, the road to recovery is much less difficult when one embraces the Spirit. The majority of my doctoral training was in developmental psychology. Almost all of the developmental theories discuss in great detail the need for homeostasis or balance in one's life. You who have seen so much pain and suffering, and so much evil, need to be able to balance that suffering and evil with a sense of goodness that exists outside of you as well as inside of you. Utilizing the spiritual dimension of your personhood and establishing a relationship with a Spirit that encompasses all goodness can be and is an incredible weapon to use against the parasite and the concomitant suffering from abuse/trauma.

## LIZ

Remember early in this book, it was stated that abuse/trauma can be abrupt or insidious. The majority of case examples that have been presented to you certainly represent situations where the abuse/trauma was abrupt or blatant and clearly visible. Sometimes abuse/trauma can be insidious or inconspicuous, but just as serious. Liz's story represents a much more insidious case of abuse/trauma. Liz, a 35-year-old married Caucasian, began counseling approximately 6 years ago and presented the following history. Liz was raised by a single mother and maternal grandparents who were quite affluent. Liz had never met her father nor was he ever talked about in her home. She described her mother as "haute and materialistic" and described her grandparents as stoic and distant. Her grandparents now were deceased, and her mother was alive and in good health.

She and her husband had been married for four years, and she felt blessed having married a good man who loved her very much. Liz and her husband had been attempting to have a child for the past two years. The couple had been treated by a fertility specialist who determined that Liz was unable to have children because of a previous existing medical condition. This reality reportedly resulted in what Liz described as a serious depression. Despite her husband's support, Liz stated that she felt inadequate as a woman and as a wife. This sense of total inadequacy would eventually lead Liz to the ultimate root of her pain. Her developmental history was factual, vague, but unremarkable. She described herself as a shy and timid child who became even more shy and timid as an adolescent. She was a straight A student throughout her elementary and secondary school years. She did participate in a few clubs in high school such as Volunteers Against Illiteracy, and Students Against Drunk Driving. She reported that she was uncomfortable in leadership roles and really was a follower. She attended a local college because of apprehensions about being away from home. She graduated summa cum laude and immediately entered the graduate program at the same college. She received her master's degree in nursing and is employed as a pediatric nurse in a local hospital.

She did not begin dating until her senior year of college. She met her husband during graduate school and the couple married shortly after they received their graduate degrees. Liz's husband was employed as an accountant at the same area hospital. Liz and her husband resided about a

10-minute drive from her mother's home, while her husband's parents resided in Philadelphia. Liz stated that her husband has two siblings and that he was very close with his brothers and parents. Liz reported she was raised in a very devout and scrupulous Christian family, and while she views herself as very spiritual, she no longer adheres to many of the teachings of her mother's church.

The focus of therapy was to assist Liz to cope with her depressive symptoms and to bolster her self-esteem. Liz appeared to be a very loving and gentle woman, but there was anger about her that was also very evident. Initially, it appeared the anger was a result of her inability to have children. But that was only a piece of the puzzle. Approximately six months into counseling, Liz was encountering some success with the stated goals, but there appeared to be something holding her back. During one session, Liz was discussing her caring for a five-year-old child who was quite ill. The child's mother, according to Liz, was parading through the hospital as if she were the mother of the year and seeking affirmation from everyone who would give it to her. Meanwhile, the child lay pitifully in her bed asking nothing more than, "Mommy, hold me." Liz went into a tirade as she related more and more of this situation. "That woman is nothing more than a damn egomaniac, feeding her ego while her child is suffering. She does not deserve to be a mother. Doesn't she see her child needs her? How can she be so self-absorbed? How can bitches like her give birth and I can't? She's a hypocritical bitch just like my mother." Liz looked at me and said, "There, now the cat's out of the bag." And indeed the cat was out of the bag. Liz related that when she was five years old, she was stricken with a severe case of psoriasis. The five-year-old was bewildered and terrified. Her mother pretended as if nothing was happening, but would constantly remind Liz to make sure she was completely covered so that no one would see her ugliness. It was late spring with school almost out for the summer, and all the other children were wearing shorts and short sleeve shirts while Liz was forced to wear long pants and long-sleeved blouses. Oh yes, and always a hat covering her beautiful hair, but also covering the red blotches on her head. And this was only the beginning of a long and painful disorder that was complicated by her mother's denial that anything could be wrong with her perfect little princess. The psoriasis was only the beginning of the neglect and the subtle emotional abuse Liz would experience from her mother.

Liz's condition was unresponsive to all the prescribed medications. Her psoriasis resulted in her becoming extremely withdrawn and shy. Her classmates were cruel and made fun of her most of the time. When she would confide in her mother as to what was happening in school, her mother would blame Liz for not trying hard enough to fit in with her classmates. The subtle but strong messages from her mother resulted in Liz becoming completely absorbed in the responsibility for her disorder and her pain. She excelled academically in order to compensate for her disorder and for being so different. Her successes went unrecognized. No matter what she did or how well she did it, the message from her mother remained the same. "You are not good enough. You are broken and damaged." Liz reported that looking back over her childhood and adolescence, a part of her felt she was neglected and abused. However, there was also a part or parts of her that negated this feeling. This part or parts of her would state, "How could you possibly say you were abused? You were never beaten. You were never sexually molested. You had a beautiful home. You never wanted for anything. Think about all those children who would have cut off their right arm to the have what you had." And yet another part would retort, "But I never felt her love. I never received any praise. I never felt good enough. I never felt lovable until I met Tim, and I do not know how long he will love me because I cannot even bear his child."

Obviously, Liz's parasite was quite shrewd in baiting her to minimize her pain and her abuse/trauma. The parasite was also very cunning in maintaining the war that raged inside of her. Rather than me explaining what Liz needed to do to become a survivor, I am going to ask you to assist her on her journey to recovery. Take what you know about abuse/trauma and the information that you have obtained from this text that you feel is important to you. Think about what would be important to Liz and begin to think about what you might say to her. You might be saying to yourself, "I do not know what to tell her. I do not know what to tell myself." My response to you is that you do know what to tell her and, by telling her, you will be telling yourself what you need to do to become a survivor. Remember, the answers and the magic do not reside in the therapist; they reside in you. From this point on, you and I will not be using the term *victim*; we will only be using the term *survivor*.

# SEVEN

## Forgiveness of the Self

The psychospiritual concept of forgiveness is both confusing and very complex. Yet it is an essential factor in the rebuilding of relationships when trust has been violated. Some people conceive forgiveness as an event, while some people confuse forgiveness with an apology or a simple "I'm sorry." Suppose you are in a grocery store and a young woman accidentally bumps you with her shopping cart. Her cart catches you right in your Achilles tendon, and you are wearing flip-flops. It really hurts. Without even making eye contact, she mumbles, "Oh, I am sorry" and proceeds on her way before you can say or do anything. I am really not sure what this might be called, but I am very sure it is obviously not within the realm of forgiveness.

Forgiveness is not only a process, but it is also a process that encompasses several key and essential steps. The first step is for one to recognize the transgression committed against another or the transgression committed against the self. The second step is to come to terms with the pain that has been caused by the commission or omission of an act or acts. Step three requires the offender to take responsibility for the act or acts and to experience, on an emotional level, both remorse and contrition. This remorse and contrition needs to be expressed directly to the offended individual or, equally important, the self. Once these steps are taken with sincerity, step four requires the offender to seek forgiveness from the person offended. It then is in the hands of the person offended as to whether he or she chooses to forgive or withhold forgiveness. If the forgiveness is granted, it is incumbent on the individual who sought the forgiveness to accept the given forgiveness and to use this for the betterment of the individual.

The most difficult step in this process is typically the acceptance and integration of the given forgiveness. Here, as you probably surmised, the parasite will engage the problematic words such as, deserving, or worthy, or several other words, to cause a rejection or distortion of the given forgiveness. Now the parasite will play both sides of the issue. The parasite will continue to reinforce the self-punishment cycle. It will taunt you with your unworthiness to accept the forgiveness and also remind you of your brokenness and sense of being damaged due to the fact that you cannot accept forgiveness. This is what I referred to as *wasted grace*. Here is yet another point where it is very important to have a connection with the Spirit or a Goodness that exists outside of you and is a reflection of the goodness that exists inside of you. Calling on this Spirit or Goodness to assist you to integrate the forgiveness of another, or the forgiveness of self, can be and often is extremely helpful and comforting.

You may be thinking, "Wait a minute, he has said time and time again that I am not responsible for my abuse/trauma. So why is he now talking about my need to forgive myself?" You raise a very good point. I'll explain. For a long time you have been involved in self-abusive behaviors. You have a part, or parts of you, that you perceived as despicable and disgusting. You may have held a part or parts of you responsible for your abuse/trauma. In an attempt to diminish your pain, you did things to yourself that were hurtful and harmful. You may have violated your own ethical or moral code with some of your behaviors. Yes, you were conned and baited by the parasite into doing these things to yourself. I know you did not know better at the time. You know you did not know better at the time. We both know the intent was to simply diminish some of the pain. Nonetheless, you abused yourself and now, in order to reduce your ego fragmentation and the splitting of your ego, you need to ask for and give forgiveness to the various parts of the self.

To begin the process of self-forgiveness, we need to reexamine stage 5, which is the splitting of emotions of sadness, guilt, and shame. As we learned, the parasite has confused your feelings of sadness with complex guilt. This complex guilt then results in you feeling responsible for your abuse/trauma. The more the parasite holds the part or parts of you responsible for your experiences, the overwhelming responsibility that you have produces a tremendous sense of shame and self-doubt. This sense of shame and self-doubt erodes your ability to trust the self. The more the parasite is able to engage you in this cyclical process, the worse you feel about yourself. What is even more dangerous about the cyclical process is that the parasite continues to draw strength and power, while you feel out of control, devastated, and hopeless. The parasite is then able to easily con you into self-destructive behaviors. Because the parasite is depleting you of psychological energy, you are less able to logically think about the consequences of your behavior, and your behaviors become more impulsive. Subsequently, the parasite then berates you with the "ridiculous, stupid, and totally negative self-destructive behaviors" that the parasite baited you into engaging in as a supposed method of self-cleansing. Figure 7.1 is an illustration of the negative cycle the parasite uses to maintain control over you. It will utilize negative cyclical processes like this in order to deplete your energy and increase your sense of hopelessness.

The two most effective weapons in breaking this cycle and thereby diminishing the parasite's power are your choosing to split the emotions of sadness and guilt, and choosing to work at forgiving yourself for any and all transgressions the parasite conned you into committing against yourself. All the sadness you feel as a result of your behaviors is logical and rational. Some of the guilt is also logical and rational. However, some of this guilt is illogical and irrational. By splitting the sadness you feel from the irrational and illogical guilt for what has happened, you will be able to diminish the burden of responsibility that you have carried for so long. This process will then afford you a considerable amount of energy

**Figure 7.1    The Parasitic Cycle of Self-Destruction**

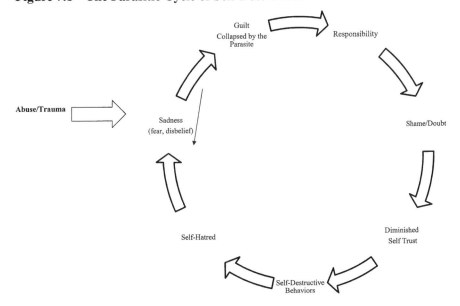

that can be used to consider the consequences of your actions and behaviors prior to engaging in them, thereby allowing you to make better choices. As you become less impulsive and actively choose more positive behaviors, you will begin to renew a sense of self-trust and begin to diminish the shame and doubt you have experienced.

For the longest time, the parasite has had you literally running around in circles with no sense of direction. The parasite has used this cyclical process to prevent you from effective problem solving. You need to keep in mind that effective problem solving is linear in nature, and not cyclical, and is goal directed. Running around in circles is nondirectional and is not goal directed, and this maintains your sense of hopelessness and helplessness, and that is exactly what the parasite wants. The more you are able to appropriately split the emotions of sadness and guilt and begin the process of forgiving yourself; you will be depleting the parasite of its energy instead of the parasite depleting you of energy. This energy then can be used for you to set a course of problem solving that is linear and goal directed. You will be able to sense the goodness that has always existed in you. The goodness the parasite has covered over by holding you accountable and responsible for your abuse/trauma. One of the best books that I have read on the topic of forgiveness is titled *Helping Clients Forgive: An Empirical Guide for Resolving Anger and Restoring Hope* by Robert Enright and Richard Fitzgibbons. While the book is primarily directed at the process of forgiving others, it can readily be adapted to the forgiveness of self. The authors define forgiving as follows:

> People upon rationally determining they have been unfairly treated, forgive when they willfully abandon resentment and related responses (to which they have a right), and endeavor to respond to the wrongdoer based on a moral principle of beneficence, which may include compassion, unconditional worth, generosity and moral love (to which the wrongdoer by nature of the hurtful act or act, has no right). (p. 24)

As you can see, this definition can easily be adapted to the concept of forgiveness of the self. The adaptation would then read: individuals upon rationally and logically coming to be truly aware that they have unfairly and self-abusively treated themselves in a convoluted effort to ease their pain, forgive the part or parts of the self as well as seek forgiveness from the part or parts of the self that they held responsible for their abuse/trauma. The individuals abandon their self-hatred and self-resentment and commit to utilizing their energies in a positive manner and to treat the self, with the assistance of the Spirit, in the fashion consistent with the ethical principle of beneficence as willed by the Spirit, which needs to include compassion, unconditional worth, respect, generosity, and kindness (not because the self is worthy or deserving of the humanities but rather because the self needs these humanities). You need to acknowledge your shortcomings and forgive the transgressions against you.

On Frankie Perez's MindGym posting, he discusses the Four Keys to Self-Acceptance. These keys are (1) friendliness, being a friend to yourself and embracing oneself; (2) love, loving oneself; (3) forgiveness, forgiving one's self; and (4) gratitude, appreciating one's self. He wrote:

> Nobel Peace Prize winner Mother Teresa of Calcutta, who dedicated her life to helping the sick and the poor refused to march against the war. "I will never do that," she said, "but as soon as you have a pro-peace rally I'll be there."
>
> The distinction that Mother Teresa made in the statement is a powerful psycho-spiritual lesson. She knew that there is a crucial difference between holding energy against versus energy for something. The energy of being against something is the consciousness of opposition, aggression and attack, while the energy of being for something is the consciousness of acceptance, forgiveness and love; one fosters war, the other peace.
>
> This psycho-spiritual lesson applies to our inner world as much as to our outer. It sheds light on those places within our consciousness where we are holding onto judgment, criticism, unkindness and lack of acceptance. Since our relationship with ourselves is at the core of our experience of inner peace, self-love, and happiness, the crucial question becomes not "what within me must I fight?" but "what within me must I love?"
>
> In my psychotherapy practice, my heart breaks every time someone tells me they are their own worst enemy, or that they sabotage or beat themselves up constantly; and this painful admission happens too often. Self criticism and condemnation have become part of the human condition. We have learned to judge ourselves with the unforgiving precision of a sniper. No outside force could ever have the sheer stamina to bring about such relentless abuse. We carry with us the negative messages we have heard during our childhood and have internalized those voices with such cruel efficiency that we are now the ones perpetrating the self abuse on a near constant basis. We tell ourselves lies that berate, undermine and break us down. Research has shown that 77% of our self talk is negative. That is 46 minutes out of every hour. Further research indicates that it takes five positive statements to counteract every negative one.
>
> It may seem hopeless and insurmountable to ever gain the upper hand on the onslaught of our own self-criticism. Yet there is a powerful and sure answer: self-acceptance.

...Forgiveness–"I forgive myself..." In order to accept ourselves we need to forgive ourselves for those judgments we are carrying against ourselves. We are constantly judging ourselves; we judge ourselves as bad, ugly, unworthy, unlovable, fat, thin, stupid...The list is endless. Some of us find it is a lot easier to be kind, compassionate, and forgiving with others, yet struggle to do so with ourselves. We perceive ourselves as unforgivable, not realizing just how arrogant it is to assume that everyone else is worthy of forgiveness but us. Forgiveness is letting go of the charges against ourselves. It is having the willingness to apply Mother Teresa's lesson of shifting from a consciousness of "against" to a consciousness "for" ourselves. (Used by permission of Frankie Perez, http://www.facebook.com/topic.php?uid=362541047781&topic=12695)

There is truly a powerful message in Mother Teresa's quote. We indeed need to use our power for forgiving ourselves. It is my sincere hope that you will use your power for your healing, and also against the parasite that has caused you so much pain and suffering. It is important to keep in mind that you are struggling against the parasite and not yourself. You are struggling for your healing, your inner peace, your goodness, and your life. Imagine a future you, who has become your own best friend. Imagine this future you, who, despite your human frailties, has come to love the self. Imagine a future you, who is genuinely grateful for the person you are. You may be saying to yourself, "I cannot even imagine what that would be like." You need to imagine this future you because through your acceptance, validation, and self-forgiveness, this is the person you are becoming.

You remember the story of Danielle, who was physically abused by her father and sexually molested by a so-called counselor in her late adolescence. After several years of therapy, Danielle was doing remarkably well. She had graduated from college, was employed in a job she loved, had celebrated two years of sobriety, and was engaged to be married. From all indications, her relationship with her fiancé was very healthy. She had transitioned to maintenance sessions, and I was seeing her approximately every two months. A few weeks after our last routine session, she called to be seen on an emergency basis. She informed me that she was not at all honest with me during our last session, and that approximately six weeks earlier, she had cheated on her fiancé. She had immediately confessed to him regarding her infidelity and was convinced he would break off the engagement. Instead of breaking off the relationship, her fiancé told her how much he loved her and that he would work at forgiving her. Danielle told me she had absolutely no idea why she was unfaithful, but it was obvious that her parasite had reared its ugly head. It appeared that as her wedding was approaching, she began to have significant self-doubts as to whether she was good enough for him. I questioned her as to what prohibited her from not sharing these feelings with her fiancé, or me, or anyone? Her response was, "I thought I was over that." Do you sense the working of the parasite in Danielle? The parasite inhibited her from sharing what were normal doubts and fears because she was supposed to be over that. The parasite baited her into believing that her fiancé was too good for her and subtly created a negative self-fulfilling prophecy. By her having the affair, she was now even more convinced that he was much too good for her. My clinical hypothesis was that this was a clear situation where the parasite baited her into self-sabotage. I asked her whether she believed her fiancé could and would truly forgive her. And she responded, "Definitely yes." Since Danielle was a deeply spiritual individual, I asked her whether her Spirit would forgive her. Again, she replied, "Yes." I then asked her whether she was willing to choose to take her fiancé's forgiveness and her Spirit's forgiveness and work at forgiving herself. She responded, "I don't believe that is possible." We then began working on how the parasite was continuing to bait her into self-sabotage by her unwillingness to work at forgiving herself. I asked Danielle how it could be that her fiancé and her Spirit would forgive her while she would not forgive herself. Was she really insinuating that her standards were higher than her fiancé's standards and her Spirit's standards? At this point in our work together, Danielle became quite indignant with me. She became angry and frustrated that I would condone such behavior and ask her to condone her behavior as well. Obviously, this was just another one of the parasite's smokescreens because the parasite could not argue the rationality of her standards being higher than her fiancé's and her Spirit's.

I needed Danielle to recognize and appreciate that I was not condoning her behavior, nor was I asking her to condone her behavior. I need you to recognize that I am not condoning, nor asking you to condone any behaviors you find offensive. I was simply asking Danielle to forgive herself. And I am asking the same of you. Danielle made a mistake. And that mistake caused both her fiancé and herself significant pain. She transgressed from her own moral and ethical boundaries. Nothing could take that back. She could not fix it and she could not undo it. What was done was done. However, her unwillingness to choose to forgive herself and her engaging in self-punishment would only serve to feed the parasite. I asked her, and I ask you, "What good will it do to simply continue to punish yourself and not choose to forgive yourself?" In the New Testament, we are told that Peter denied the Christ three times and that Judas betrayed the Christ.

Reportedly, Peter wept with sorrow and contrition, and Judas hanged himself. It is been said by theologians that Judas's real sin was not the betrayal of the Christ, but rather his belief that he could not be forgiven and therefore he took his own life as an ultimate form of self-punishment. I ask you not to make the same mistake. Seek the forgiveness of the Spirit with the belief that the forgiveness has already been granted. Work at integrating this forgiveness and do not allow it to become wasted grace.

Danielle could not pretend it did not happen, but she could choose to forgive what had happened. It is a true struggle for her but her guilt is diminishing, and she is becoming more accepting of her now husband's forgiveness and her Spirit's forgiveness. My continued hope for her is that she comes to fully accept her human shortcomings and eventually completely forgives herself.

The concept of the Spirit has appeared several times in this chapter. You may recall Beth's story in the very powerful statement she made to me regarding her Spirit. She stated that perhaps she needed to forgive her Spirit, and perhaps, even more importantly, her understanding or misunderstanding of her Spirit. I have heard people say how much they hate their Spirit. In reality, they are saying they hate their misunderstanding of the Spirit. The important aspect to note here is that these people who say they hate the Spirit, whether they realize it or not, are talking about the relationship they have with their Spirit. Anger, frustration, even hatred are normal reactions when a loved one disappoints us by an action or inaction. You may be furious or even hate the Spirit, who did not seem to be there to rescue you from your abuse/trauma. Do not be afraid to communicate your feelings to the Spirit. The reality is that this omnipotent Spirit already knows your feelings perhaps better than you do. Do you need to work on forgiving your understanding or your misunderstanding of your Spirit? Do you need to forgive the Spirit for not rescuing you from your pain and suffering? Do you need to forgive the Spirit for allowing someone to abuse you? Do what is necessary to rectify your relationship with your Spirit.

We have already examined Josephine's story. What we have not discussed is her struggle to forgive herself. Her forgiveness of herself has been a long and difficult battle. What she continues to hold against herself is the continued belief that she was, as she phrased it, a "neglectful mother." What is really helping Josephine is her choosing to alter her perception of herself as a mother. The more she recognizes her goodness, the less guilt she is experiencing. She is becoming very good at splitting sadness and guilt, and embracing the reality that she did the best she could in raising her children. Josephine has a wonderful sense of humor and comments often that I told her she needed to forgive herself at roughly the fifth or sixth session. She will routinely comment on how much money she could have saved if she had only listened to me back then. This is in part why she wanted her story told. Because she realizes how much energy she wasted on beating herself up because she was unwilling to forgive herself. Josephine would definitely agree with Frankie Perez's statement that we certainly can be our own worst enemy. She wanted her story told because she is living proof that one does not have to remain victim but can truly become a survivor when one chooses to become a survivor. After 50 plus years of suffering and struggling with her parasite, Josephine is a true survivor.

Up to this point in the chapter we examined only the forgiveness of the self and have not even mentioned forgiving the abuser(s). Many authors on the subject of abuse/trauma and many clinicians who treat survivors propose the need to forgive the abuser(s). They would argue that forgiving the abuser(s) is a way for the survivor to diminish the valid anger, frustration, and perhaps even hatred they feel for their abuser. Encouraging the survivor to forgive the abuser(s) is then actually directed at helping the survivors. It is important to recognize how much anger, frustration, and even hatred you carry with you and to recognize what those negative feelings are doing to you. There are also many authors and clinicians who espouse the hang-them-high attitude. I am not proposing either approach. Rather, my approach to the question, "Do I need to forgive the abuser?" is focused on what you need for your healing. Some of my patients needed to forgive their abuser, while the majority of my patients would not even consider forgiving their abuser. What is important is that you go back to the definition presented earlier in this text and keep in mind what Enright and Fitzgibbons have stated, in particular your right to the resentment and other feelings you may have. Furthermore, you need to keep in mind the statement, "to which the wrongdoer by nature of the hurtful act or acts has no right." You need to look deep inside and ascertain what is best for you. From a spiritual vantage point, I believe my Spirit's ability to forgive is unlimited. However, while the Spirit's forgiveness is bountiful, one must first ask for the Spirit's forgiveness in order to be forgiven. I am certainly not a theologian and I might not be theologically sound on this position, but I believe in the "If you do not ask for forgiveness, you do not get forgiveness" approach.

I know that my experiences are limited to the patients I have treated. However, to date, I have yet to treat a survivor who has been asked by his or her abuser for forgiveness. If you have been asked by your abuser for forgiveness and you believe it will aid you in your healing, then I would encourage you to work at forgiving the abuser. If you have not been asked for forgiveness by the abuser, but believe you need to forgive your abuser in order to promote your own healing, I would then encourage you to work at forgiving the abuser because this is what you need to do to promote your healing. Again, you need to do what is best for you. No matter what course of action you choose regarding your abuser, the forgiveness of the self is an even more crucial issue and therefore you need to focus all your energies on forgiving yourself before attending to the issue of forgiving the abuser.

There are two words that we need to never associate with forgiveness. One is to forget; the other is to condone. How many times in our lives have we heard the phrase "forgive and forget?" The reality is that even when we choose to forgive, we do not forget. There are many things that have happened to me in my lifetime. I have chosen to work at forgiving many of them. However, I have not forgotten a single one of them. Unfortunately, there are also many times when I have hurt other individuals. Experiencing appropriate guilt, and with great remorse, I have asked for forgiveness and then been given the blessings of forgiveness. Still, accepting, embracing, and integrating that forgiveness and forgiving myself have remained a difficult task, especially when I listen to my parasite. When our daughter, who is now in her 30s, was less than a year old, she slipped and fell in the bathtub. She wanted a bubble bath, and I was the one bathing her. The bubble bath solution was somewhat oily. At one point she stood up, and I remember saying "No, baby" and attempted to stop her from slipping and falling. She slipped through my arms and hit the rim of the bathtub so hard that she drove her two front teeth back up into her gum. For years, this little girl went through dental procedure after dental procedure. Today she has beautiful teeth and a beautiful smile and, yes, I am biased. I myself have worked for years on splitting my emotions of sadness and guilt. I have worked very hard to forgive myself even though I know I did nothing wrong and am not responsible for her falling. However, that horrible scene still flashes in my head and it is probably a scene I will carry to my grave. It is a scene I wish I could forget, but the reality is that it is part of my history.

The second word that is not a part of forgiving is the word condone. As you recall, Danielle was very concerned that I was condoning her behavior and asking her to likewise condone her behavior. Many times people believe that when we accept something as a fact we are also condoning that fact. This is completely inaccurate. As a clinician, I must accept the fact that abuse/trauma exists. Let me be very clear that while I accept this fact, I do not condone abuse/trauma, nor do I excuse the behavior of the abuser. When I speak of forgiving yourself, I am not suggesting you condone or simply excuse your behavior. What is wrong is wrong. Yet, to endlessly self-punish for a wrong that has been committed either against another or against the self, in reality, serves no purpose. Self-abuse does not make a wrong right. Self-abuse does not make amends to another or to the self. Forgiving yourself is not condoning your act of commission or omission, but does call you to task to learn from your mistake and to commit to working at not replicating this mistake.

Before we leave this chapter, it might be very important to you for us to discuss the story of Alisha. At the time I began working with Alisha, she was a college sophomore who came to the counseling center for assistance with anxiety and her difficulty with friendships. She reported that she had been in and out counseling since she was in the seventh grade. Her parents had been married for 21 years and had what she thought was a very healthy relationship until 2 years ago when her father announced he was leaving her mother. Alisha stated that she was devastated by the thought of her parents being divorced. She was an only child and she reported that she was always closer to her dad than her mother. "It seemed like no matter what I did, I was never good enough and I could never please her. Last semester, I made the Dean's list with a grade point average of 3.8. But that was not good enough for my mother."

Alisha reported that her father was transferred by his employer after she completed the fifth grade. Up until that time, she was in the public school system and had made many friends and was doing well academically. According to Alisha, the school system where her father was transferred to did not have a very good reputation, so her parents enrolled her in a private school. She found the transition to private school to be extremely difficult and did not seem to fit in with the other children and had great difficulty making friends. About halfway through the school year, Alisha was invited to a birthday party by one of the most popular girls in class. Alisha and her parents were elated with the prospect she finally might be able to make some friends. When she arrived at the party, the other girls immediately started to pick on her and make fun of her. The girl who invited Alisha informed her that she invited her to be "our entertainment for the party." The girls started pushing and shoving Alisha and Alisha shoved back. At some point in this shoving match, the birthday girl fell and cut her hand. The birthday girl went screaming to her mother and told her Alisha pushed her for no reason. The mother told Alisha to call her parents and get out of her house immediately. When Alisha's mother picked her up, Alisha attempted to explain to her mother what happened, but her mother kept asking Alisha what she did to cause the girls to attack her with such violence. Alisha's hurt and sadness, compounded by her mother's minimization of the abuse/trauma and the mother's indirect blaming of her daughter, enabled Alisha's parasite to immediately absorb the guilt, the responsibility, and the shame.

Alisha continued to be bullied for the next few months, and she became quite depressed and angry. Alisha reports that she became very aggressive and was constantly in fights. Her grades fell drastically, until finally her parents agreed to allow her to transfer to a public school. Unfortunately, Alisha took her aggression to her new school and was eventually required to enter into counseling. Alicia reported that the counselors she had seen throughout the years told her time and time again that she needed to get over the bullying she had experienced. No one seemed to comprehend that for Alisha the bullying was definitely a form of abuse/trauma. Alisha reported that somewhere in her mid-high school years, she curtailed her aggression, but began allowing herself to be used like a doormat. As you can see, Alisha first turned her hurt and anger outward, which was very problematic. However, as she curtailed her external aggression, she simply turned her hurt and anger against herself, which was equally problematic.

Alisha finally received the validation she so desperately needed and began to understand how the parasite had played her to assume the guilt, the responsibility, the shame, and the sense of being damaged. Once Alisha began to accept her abuse/trauma as an unchangeable and began to internalize the validation, she immediately set on a course to forgive herself. Alisha, who is an education major, would talk to the various parts of her as if she were talking to the classroom of elementary children. She would report that she would explain to these younger parts of herself exactly what happened and the irrationality of assuming any guilt, responsibility, or shame. Toward the end of the spring semester, Alisha reported that she sincerely believed that she had made great headway in forgiving herself. She stated, "It is like having a coach in your head all the time. The coach acknowledges the things you do well and sometimes encourages you to do things differently. I know I can continue to replace my parasite with my coach."

I have included Alisha's story for several reasons. The first reason for presenting her story is that it reinforces the notion that the answer to what you need to do in order to bring about healing lies inside of you. After working on stages 1 and 2, Alisha immediately knew that she needed to work on the forgiveness of self stage. Quite honestly, I did not and would not have had a sufficient knowledge of her to recommend immediately addressing the self-forgiveness stage to her. The important point is that she knew, and I believe, like Alisha, you know. The second reason is to illustrate just how life-giving forgiveness of the self is and can be. The third reason is to illuminate the reality that bullying is definitely a situation of abuse/trauma.

I genuinely hope that I have been able to convince you of the necessity of self-forgiveness. The inhibition of self-forgiveness can be and often is one of the last stands your parasite can make in your war. Keep in mind the parasite is cunning, shrewd, and baffling. Do not let the parasite con you into continuing the war because you refuse to work at forgiving yourself. You know how to forgive others. Use that knowledge, caring, and compassion to forgive someone who desperately needs it, *you*.

# EIGHT

## Perfectionism and People-Pleasing

The concepts of perfectionism and people-pleasing have been mentioned in the chapter on development. However, both my research and treatment of survivors of abuse have convinced me that these dynamic concepts play a significant parasitic role in maintaining the self-abuse cycle. Unless these concepts are understood and given boundaries, the parasite will continue to use these dynamic aspects to thwart healing.

One of the most common traits of people who have experienced abuse/trauma is their drive toward perfectionism. Since I have not had the privilege of meeting you and/or evaluating you, I cannot say that you are a perfectionist. You might be saying to yourself, "He obviously does not know me, because if he did he would never say I am a perfectionist. I am anything but a perfectionist." I have heard statements like these most of my career. All my patients have said the very same things. I am not saying that you think you are perfect. You know your human shortcomings all too well. Please, listen to what I am saying and be honest with yourself. Perhaps defining the term will help. The *APA Dictionary of Psychology* defines perfectionism as "the tendency to demand of others or oneself a higher level of performance than is required by the situation, thought by some to be a risk factor for depression." Perfectionism should not be confused with an obsessive-compulsive disorder. Perfectionism also should not be confused with individuals who believe they are perfect, which is commonly viewed as narcissism. Narcissism is "excessive self-love and egocentrism." I know that does not describe you.

Typically survivors of abuse/trauma have come to believe what the parasite has been telling them for years. The sense of being damaged and/or broken has resulted in the survivor believing that he or she is something less than the majority of people. Survivors believe they need to be perfect in order to compensate for being damaged, broken, dirty, and disgusting. Inside, the parasite has been saying things such as, "You do not deserve to be her friend. You are not worthy to be in their company. You cannot marry him; he is much too good for you." And within the statements, the parasite plays the "if they only knew" game. Bill Zeller's parasite, which he called the darkness, played this game well. His parasite kept telling him that he was nothing more than an animal, and perhaps it was better that he take his life before others found out. As is obvious, this if they only knew game can be very dangerous and deadly. I customarily shake hands with patients, male or female, as they exit my office, except in those situations where it is culturally and religiously inappropriate. For one young man, this common human gesture of courtesy became a significant source of distress. Tony is a 29-year-old man who was abused physically and emotionally throughout his childhood and adolescence by his alcoholic mother. He was abandoned at birth by his biological father. At the end of our fourth session, I stretched out my hand to shake Tony's hand. He put his head down and said, "Please do not ask me to shake your hand; I am too dirty inside to shake your hand." In the practice of psychology, one has a tendency to hear many shocking things, but I was very taken aback by his statement and the pain that was visible in his eyes. Tony, who felt too dirty on the inside to shake my hand, was a true perfectionist.

Survivors who are perfectionists tend to be very compassionate toward others. They are typically very understanding of others' human frailties and have an incredible ability to forgive others. However, when it comes to them, they are relentless in the demands they place on themselves. There is no understanding, no compassion, and no forgiveness for the self. Perfectionists could receive 99 compliments and one slight criticism in a given week. Can you guess where they focus all their attention? Where do you focus your attention? Is this beginning to sound more like you? Are you a perfectionist? How do you cope with compliments? How do you cope with positive accomplishments? How do you cope with success? Do you ever take a compliment, an accomplishment, or a success and allow yourself to really feel positive about yourself? Or do these positives just seem to bounce off you? How do you cope with anything negative? Does it seem to just stick to you like Velcro? How long do you churn this negativity inside of you? Do you churn for hours, days, or weeks? Are you ever able to let it go? Do you see how the parasite plays these things against you? No wonder you truly feel broken, damaged, and less than everyone else. You are striving for perfection, and your demands on the self provide the parasite with an incredible and continuous source of energy that it uses against you. Perfectionism creates a negative paradoxical effect: the harder you work at doing everything right, the more you see what is wrong. My wife is a perfectionist. If you were to compliment her on how clean our home is, she will proceed to show you all the dust. She might even open our junk drawer just to demonstrate how messy she is. If you compliment her on her dress, she will proceed to show you every pull in the fabric then tell you she paid seven dollars for it at Kmart.

Perfectionists have a tendency to catastrophize their human shortcomings. A tiny pimple on your forehead feels as if you are growing another head. Your new car has a tiny, almost unnoticeable scratch on the driver's door, and to you it feels as if your car has been demolished. You spill a glass of water and to you it feels as if you flooded your apartment. You go to the funeral home and become so nervous and upset that you thank the family for coming. You are now convinced you are the dumbest jackass ever created. And it only gets worse. Because you judge yourself as being inferior, you set unrealistic goals for yourself. These unrealistic goals become negative self-fulfilling prophecies doomed to failure. As you fail in the goals you have established, you continue to add more evidence regarding your inferiority. The parasite then uses this negative energy to bait you into establishing even higher goals in order to compensate for your inferiority. Like we have seen in other situations, the parasite keeps you involved in a cyclical process that keeps you spinning and prevents you from any attainment of your goals. Can you see the self-sabotaging process the parasite has created?

One goal that perfectionists typically adopt is the drive to people-please. The goal is to please everyone all the time. The parasite has baited you into believing that if you can please everyone all the time that you will surely compensate for your inferiority, for being damaged or broken, and for being dirty or disgusting. I would like to give you an example from Tony's story. Despite the abuse that Tony has suffered from his mother, he was desperately entrenched in an obligation to please her. Tony's fiancée, who knew his history, has a significant dislike for Tony's mother. During the Christmas holidays, Tony decided that it would be a wonderful thing for him to take his fiancée and his mother out to dinner and a movie. Both Tony's fiancée and his mother reluctantly agreed to Tony's plan. During this quite elaborate dinner at a very expensive restaurant, Tony's mother made some derogatory remarks to his fiancée. Tony was shocked and speechless and unfortunately said nothing. His fiancée became furious and left the table. Tony, now recovering from the shock of his mother's comments, said something to his mother who also became furious and left the restaurant. The situation occurred some time ago; however, Tony is still lamenting the situation. In his perception of the situation, and compounded with the fact that his mother and fiancée are still quite angry with him, the Christmas disaster was totally his fault. The question I would ask you is, "Do you believe it is completely Tony's fault and Tony's responsibility for the Christmas disaster?" Is it always your fault and are you always completely responsible?

It is important to note that despite the incredible pain suffered at the hands of the abuser, survivors typically remain bonded to their abuser especially if the abuser is a parent. If you find yourself in a similar situation to Tony, do not allow the parasite to use this bond as evidence of your weakness or your stupidity. It is a very common occurrence and, as we discussed in the developmental section, very understandable.

Tony's parasite played on both his perfectionism and his people-pleasing, and the result is that Tony feels as if he is a complete failure. The parasite has even further baited him to take full responsibility for the disastrous evening. He now contends that he must somehow do something for both his mother and his fiancée to compensate for the disaster that he caused. What assistance can we provide to Tony to help him perceive the situation in a more logical and rational manner? What assistance can I provide to you to help you perceive your situations in a more logical and rational manner? Perhaps it would help to examine some of the erroneous beliefs that you and Tony might have.

In the scheme of relationships, are we responsible for the actions of others? Parents need to be responsible for their young children. However, in order to grow into healthy adults, the children eventually need to begin to assume the responsibility for themselves. Certainly by mid to late adolescence, individuals need to be responsible for their behavior. Suppose my son, at age five, throws a baseball and accidentally smashes the neighbor's window, I as the parent am responsible. Is it appropriate for me to take the same responsibility when he is of age 12? I believe you are agreeing with me that the answer is no. In our relationships as adults, I believe we are responsible to one another not for one another. This change in prepositions (to versus for) is not just a semantic change. Rather, it is a powerful mindset alteration and can assist us in perceiving our responsibility from a more logical and rational standpoint. In our relationships, we obviously impact one another both positively and negatively. But does this impact then make us responsible for others and what they subsequently do or do not do? I think not. Suppose my wife and I had a terrible argument last evening and I am still hurt and angry the next day. Is she responsible for my abrupt behavior to my patients or to my students because I am still hurt and angry and offended by her behavior? I have a sense that you would not hold her responsible for my behavior. Many of my patients have recovered from their abuse/trauma and some have not recovered. Am I responsible for their successes and their failures? Just as I cannot take the credit for their successes, I cannot take the responsibility for their failures. I need to be responsible to them but I cannot be held responsible for them. Similarly, Tony is not responsible for his mother's crudeness. Here is where the parasite collapsed the emotions of sadness and guilt. Tony had every right to be quite sad regarding his mother's behavior toward his fiancée. He was also saddened that his mother hurt his fiancée, but the emotion of guilt in this situation is illogical and irrational. He did not cause his mother's outburst. Even if he had provoked her into making a crude comment, he would still not be responsible for his mother's action. He did nothing wrong. Was he completely responsible to protect his fiancée from his mother's crudeness? I have said to Tony perhaps he needed to support his fiancée in this situation. However, she is an adult and as an adult needed to address the situation as well. Granted, it was a very awkward situation for his fiancée. I do not perceive that there was anything that Tony could have done to prevent the situation. Tony's parasite insisted that there was something he could have done to prevent the situation, and regrettably this parasite was more convincing than me. Tony may need to come to terms with the fact that his mother and his fiancée will never become best friends. That is really up to both of them.

For as long as Tony could remember, his mother had told him that she was totally miserable all her life and that is the reason why she drank. She also told him that it was his responsibility to make her happy. The parasite, using Tony's complete lack of boundaries regarding his perfectionism and people-pleasing, baited him into wanting to do the impossible. No one can take responsibility for another's happiness. My wife is not responsible for my happiness. She can do and does many, many things to please me; however, it is my responsibility to make myself happy, and it is her responsibility to please herself. And it is no one's responsibility to do this perfectly. Tony might derive a sense of peace as well as a sense of power from the serenity prayer we discussed earlier. Tony cannot change another person, but he can alter his own perceptions and his subsequent behaviors.

Tony needs to accept he is a perfectionist as well as a people pleaser. He needs to accept the reality that these aspects of his personality are positive qualities when and if he maintains appropriate and consistent boundaries on these qualities. He needs to accept himself and those around him as imperfect human beings. Tony needs to alter his expectations of himself and others. The parasitic "I should please my mother" needs to become a reality-based "I wish I could please my mother." He can wish that his mother and his fiancée will become friends, but he cannot realistically expect that he can make this happen. Expecting that he can make this happen will only serve to provide the parasite with ample energy to maintain a cycle of self-abuse and self-sabotage. Tony needs to alter how he treats himself so he can say before his Spirit, "I did my best. It was far from enough but it was my best." When he can say this with sincerity, he will be able to give himself the same compassion, understanding, and forgiveness that he freely gives to others. Alfred Adler, a theorist I have mentioned previously, believed that the drive for perfection or superiority was simply a compensation for the feelings of inferiority. Adler also believed "the healthy person is the one who has the courage to be human." When one embraces their imperfections, they are also embracing imperfection as a given factor of being human (Murdock, 2009).

There is also a more subtle difficulty that can be encountered on an interpersonal level when an individual does not contain his or her perfectionism and people-pleasing. If you are going to make everything perfect on an interpersonal level and please everyone, you are going to need a significant amount of control. You will need to control every aspect of what happens in a particular situation, and you will also need to control the behavior of all the participants involved in this situation. In essence, you will need to control that everyone in the sandbox plays nice. The question is how do you do that? You will need for everyone to do exactly what you expect them to do. True, you have the best of intentions, but, as stated previously, the road to hell is paved with good intentions. The individuals that you have involved in this particular situation may become quite angry and resentful when you exercise a subtle but significant amount of control in the situation. Imagine this: You want to invite your entire family for Thanksgiving. You have this image of a perfect family holiday. Everyone is seated around the table as you present the magnificent turkey that you have cooked. Everyone is in awe of the wonderful meal you prepared, and how splendid the table is set. Oh yes, and did I mention that everyone is healthy and happy and is so glad to see one another? Did I mention that everyone in the family not only loves one another, but really likes one another? Did I also mention that there was not a single crude comment made during the entire day? Did I also mention that no one got drunk? I am sure by now that you are getting the point and perceiving the impossibility of the perfect Thanksgiving holiday. How could you ever have the kind of control necessary to make a perfect Thanksgiving holiday? Obviously, the reality is that you cannot ever have this kind of control. Do you see how the parasite can play havoc with the best of intentions? We have discussed how your parasite plays you. Keep in mind, everyone has a parasite. Their parasite is playing them. Sometimes it can be an incredibly painful mess that only serves to increase your sense of inferiority and your self-directed anger and frustration because of your inferiority.

Trish is a 56-year-old divorced woman who has two adult daughters aged 36 and 33. Trish is the oldest of seven children, and she was physically and emotionally abused by her biological father and mother. She has no recall of any of her childhood below the age of 10 except for the hands, the belts, and shoes from which she suffered the physical abuse. Trish reported that at the age of 20 she married the first man she had ever dated. "I did not know love because I never felt love. I just felt damaged and was so happy that someone told me I was pretty and that they wanted to be with me. I was in love with being in love." The man she married was unfortunately quite abusive. She has been in counseling for the past 10 years and was able to terminate this abusive relationship after many years of abuse. Trish has made incredible progress regarding her perfectionism and people-pleasing tendencies. One particular disastrous incident in her life that actually served to help her alter her perception of herself and reduce her people-pleasing and perfectionism tendencies involved her desire to have the perfect family vacation. She invited both her daughters and her sons-in-laws and her grandchildren to go to Disney World. It was going to be the perfect family vacation. However, Trish's daughters did not really get along with each other, nor did their husbands get along with each other. Trish had hoped that this vacation would help her bond with her daughters and would also help her daughters and husbands to bond with each other. Trish had imagined walking through Disney World as a family and enjoying one another's company as well as enjoying the grandchildren's delight at being at Disney. That did not happen. Everyone wanted to go a different way. No one was willing to compromise. The more Trish attempted to control her family's behaviors, the more they resisted and the angrier they became with her. She spent most of the family vacation in tears and alone. By the time she came home from vacation, she was so depressed that she admitted to thoughts of suicide. The parasite had taken her perceived failure with the family vacation and reinforced just how damaged this woman was. Thankfully, Trish was finally able to see the impossibility of being perfect and pleasing everyone all the time. She has been gradually able to rebuild her relationship with both daughters and believes that the lessons learned from this disastrous vacation has aided her in containing much of her perfectionism and people-pleasing tendencies. Trish's strong spiritual base and her connection with the Spirit have enabled her to forgive herself for her human shortcomings. She wanted her story told because she wanted to give you hope that you can place appropriate boundaries on the strong tendencies of perfectionism and people-pleasing. And she wanted you to know how helpful it was for her to turn to the Spirit to give her strength to forgive herself for being human.

I want to reiterate that the drives for perfectionism and people-pleasing are not unhealthy per se. Your drive for perfection has enabled you to succeed in many positive ways. Your perfectionism kept you going in your darkest days. Your striving to be perfect did not let you give into the parasite even before you knew that it was the parasite. Personally my drive for perfection enabled me to obtain my doctorate and with the help of the Spirit to complete this text. Similarly, my people-pleasing drive has assisted me in becoming a kind, compassionate, and caring man. No, the drives of perfectionism and people-pleasing are not necessarily dysfunctional characteristics. They can and do provide us with psychological energy necessary to succeed. Nonetheless, if these energy sources are not properly contained or do not have appropriate boundaries, they can lead to a meltdown. Consider a nuclear power plant. A nuclear power plant uses highly radioactive material and creates a nuclear reaction. This reaction, when properly contained, is an incredible source of energy. If it is not properly contained, a meltdown can occur and a meltdown can be tremendously devastating. In an analogous manner, these characteristics of perfectionism and people-pleasing need to be properly contained.

Developmental psychologists have researched and theorized regarding the importance of homeostasis or balance to healthy human functioning. You know that your abuse/trauma caused a significant disruption in your sense of homeostasis or balance. The parasite has continued to use this sense of disruption in your homeostasis against you. Healthy functioning requires us to develop a sense of balance between the polarities that exist in our world. These polarities include, but are not limited to, good or bad, black or white, trust or no trust, caring too much or not caring at all, inferior or superior. While you need to develop a sense of balance between these polarities, the parasite inhibits you from developing this balance through what is known as dichotomous thinking. The *APA Dictionary of Psychology* defines the dichotomous thinking as "the tendency to think in terms of bipolar opposites, that is, in terms of the best and worst, without accepting the possibilities that lie between these two extremes." Unfortunately, we do not live in a black-white world, and in many situations we need to find the gray in the situations. But, in order to find the gray, we need to trust in ourselves and in others. Your abuse/trauma violated your trust in yourself and in others, and this is how the parasite maintains the dichotomous polarized thinking. Many times, it perhaps feels as if you are on a teeter-totter up or down, down or up, but never somewhere in between these polarities. While I do not wish to be completely redundant, it is critical that you perceive how important it is for you to build or rebuild the trust that has been violated.

Perhaps, throughout your life, you have experienced near meltdowns or actual meltdowns. My vision of a meltdown is when the perfectionist or people pleaser says to himself or herself, "That is it. I am through pleasing others. Screw everybody. I am done with people. I am done with trying to make them happy. Now it is my turn. I am going to do what I want when I want." Actually this is not really you talking; it is the parasite baiting you to swing to the opposite polarity. If you recall, this is exactly where Alisha started out, only to eventually swing to the other polarity. Neither of these extremes is helpful; in fact, the extremes or polarities can be very harmful. Operating from this negative polarity only serves to create more guilt in you over time. You felt angry, frustrated, and resentful when you were striving for perfection and making others happy at your own expense. Now that you have moved to the other polarity of pleasing only yourself, the guilt feelings you are now experiencing are much worse. The parasite will eventually bait you into swinging back to the opposite polarity, only now you must work even harder to be perfect in pleasing others in order to compensate for your wayward ways. The parasitic cycle continues in your striving for the impossible while never really embracing the reality that these goals are impossible.

In order to place appropriate boundaries on your perfectionism and people-pleasing, you need to begin to balance your strengths against your human weaknesses. I have already expressed to you the importance of taking an inventory of your strengths as proposed in stage 3. You need to come to terms with the fact that you are not inferior to other people because of your abuse/trauma. In fact, your ability to cope with the abuse/trauma seems to me to make you somewhat superior to others because you are a survivor who is able to cope with significant adversity and tragedy. This is an interesting point, is it not? Please, ponder this point for a while. Do not just blow it off. You will need to work at learning to accept compliments. You will also need to work to refrain the parasite from negating them in your head with the parasitic "but" and "if you only knew" comments. Simply say, "Thank you." Be aware of how the parasite will attempt to negate these compliments by using the conjunction "but." For example, "Yes, I am a kind person, but I am damaged." The list of the statements could go on and on almost forever. If you find it extremely difficult to eliminate the "but," I would ask you to simply alter the placement of the positive and the negative. By that I mean, placing the negative first and then using the "but" to negate it with the positive. Research into mental functioning informs us that there are some very powerful results that can be derived from doing this. Do you perceive the difference between these next two statements? "I am damaged, but I am a kind person." "I have many human frailties, but I am a strong and courageous person." Do you see the difference? Is this something you choose to work at doing? These things really do work. I hope you work at them.

As you become more comfortable with simply accepting compliments, you then need to begin to integrate these compliments so that you do not just hear them in your head, you feel them in your soul. I have often asked my patients to take these compliments and successes and to visualize making a deposit in their heart bank. When you make a deposit in the heart bank or integrate the compliment or success, it actually acts as a reserve for those times when life becomes really difficult. Whenever I receive notes from patients or students that are complimentary, I save them in a particular file. During really low points in my life when I get down on myself, I will take this file out and read some of them. Believe it or not, it really does help. Please give this a chance. The only thing you have to lose is some of your pain.

We all make audio and/or video tapes in our heads. These tapes are a part of our learning process and can be used to help us solve problems. In stressful times, these tapes can play over and over again in our head. Tony played the tape of his dinner with his mom and fiancé numerous times. Instead of helping him resolve the problem, Tony's parasite kept him reviewing the tape because the parasite insisted that Tony had done something wrong. Here is yet another example of the parasite's manipulation of Tony to attempt to make sense where no sense existed. This is common with the parasite. It will manipulate you into multiple reviews of the tape based on the negative self-filling prophesy that you did something wrong and that it could have been prevented. You, similar to Tony, keep reviewing the tape until you identify what you did wrong. I would ask you to adopt the three and out method of reviewing tapes of problematic situations. If after the third review you are not able to ascertain what you did or might have done to cause or alter the situation, you stop the reviews. This is similar to the hunt for the evil where, at some point, you need to simply stop hunting for the evil or the error because the evil or error is just not there. You might work at turning the no sense situation over to the Spirit.

You will also need to work at fully accepting that many of your goals may be impossible and strive for containment of these drives of perfectionism and people-pleasing. I know too well that I cannot tell you to lower your standards. That is not what I am suggesting. I am simply suggesting that you recognize how high the bar is that you have set for yourself. I know you will not lower the bar. Work at being compassionate and forgiving to yourself when you cannot clear the bar because perhaps where you have set the bar, no one can. I have used the word containment several times, and it is important that you know what I mean by this term. Containment is the establishment of appropriate limits and/or boundaries. I know that your trust has been violated. You know rebuilding your self-trust is not easy, but do you know it is not impossible. You not only have a right but also a responsibility to establish or reestablish boundaries. You need to be able to say no to things you do not want to do. You need to be able to say no when others attempt to take advantage of you. You need to have a life. You need to know you are not a doormat. Boundaries are critical factors in healing and are also essential to healthy functioning. They afford us with a sense of control over ourselves and our behavior. After all, controlling ourselves and our behavior is really the only control we have in our lives. The next chapter will explore the concept of boundaries in depth.

# NINE

## Boundaries

Due to the importance of boundaries to you the survivor, this section may be a bit technical but it is very important that you understand the concepts. At points, it might also seem a bit redundant as you and I begin to tie numerous points of this text together. If you have read other texts on the effects of childhood or adolescence abuse/trauma, or you are currently in counseling, I am quite certain that you have heard the words boundaries, boundary violations, appropriate boundaries, and/or limit setting. Similar to homeostasis, boundaries are yet another essential aspect of healthy psychological functioning. Boundaries are crucial to our basic human needs of safety and security, and therefore critical in the development of a sense of trust of both self and others.

The use of the definition of boundaries will hopefully provide some clarity. The *APA Dictionary of Psychology* defines a boundary as "a psychological demarcation that protects the integrity of an individual or group or that helps the person or group set realistic limits on participation in a relationship or activity." It is important that we examine this definition more closely. "A demarcation that protects" speaks directly to the notion of safety and security. Abraham Maslow (1954) in his book *Motivation and Personality* established a well-accepted theory regarding basic human needs. Maslow described needs as being similar to a pyramid wherein the most essential human needs such as food, water, clothing, and shelter were at the bottom of the pyramid. Without these needs being met, an individual cannot survive. When you are starving to death or dying of thirst, you certainly are not thinking about or working toward self-actualization. Your entire energies are obviously devoted to getting some food or some water. Maslow established the second level of needs to be safety and security. If you do not have a sense of safety and security, you cannot move to the next level, which is a sense of love and belonging. What Maslow was saying was that you cannot move up the pyramid until the needs of the particular level you are on are satisfied. In essence, you can become fixated at a particular need level until that need is satisfied. You will need to establish or reestablish demarcations that protect your safety and security. This is essential to your recovery. These demarcations will enable you to establish realistic limits of both yourself and others.

We humans are very particular about our boundaries. If you own a home, I am sure you know the demarcation of your property boundaries. Some of our boundaries are more rigid than others. I am certain that if you invited me to your home for dinner and you found me rummaging through your bedroom drawers, you might be very upset. If I responded to your protests in very cavalier manner, I think you might be even more upset. You and I both need people to respect our boundaries. How uncomfortable do you become in a crowded elevator? How uncomfortable would you become if only you and I were on the elevator and I was figuratively standing on top of you. Social psychologists would explain to you that discomfort you are experiencing is a result of a violation of your spatial territory. Typically, we require at least three feet of space between us and people we do not know well. Consider the incredible discomfort and pain you experienced when someone violated the boundaries of your mind, your heart, your body, and your soul. Consider the horrific pain you experienced having your sense of safety and security crushed. Consider the compounding pain and suffering you experienced with the cavalier attitude the abuser had when he or she was violating your boundaries, as if the abuser had a right to violate your boundaries. You know too well how this violation impacted your ability to trust others and, more importantly, your ability to trust yourself. The trauma of abuse lies in the boundary violation.

The boundary violation is the result of a breach in the child's or adolescent's sense of safety and security, which results in the feeling of a complete loss of control in the child or adolescent. This feeling of a loss of control is intense and completely unbalances the child's or adolescent's sense of internal stability and homeostasis. The child, unaware of the fact that one cannot make sense of nonsense, begins to make sense of the abuse/trauma in order to regain equilibrium and homeostasis. Here is where the parasite is able to gain incredible power and it begins to infect the various parts of the ego and to play them against one another. Listen to the power in the following statements:

"You are a lazy sack of shit. I wish we never had you."

"I would not have to drink, if I have a son I could be proud of. But no, I got you."

"I did not want to beat you, but you had to push me. You are nothing but a stupid little bastard."

"This is how little girls love their daddy. Don't you love daddy? Don't you like making daddy feel good?"

"This is how God wants me to show you love."

"I should have aborted you when I had the chance."

"I cursed the day we adopted you. Your own biological mother did not want you. Do you know why? Well, I do. You are a slimy piece of garbage that should never have been born."

Can you see all the contaminants that the child absorbs creating the infection of the parasite? Can you see all the power the parasite gets from these horrible statements? Can you see how the parasite will cause the child or adolescent to collapse the sadness into guilt and absorb both the pain and the responsibility? Gestalt theory has postulated the concept of introjections to aid us in understanding what and how children or adolescents learn about themselves and their world. This concept of introjections is also very helpful in providing us with a framework of how the child could absorb the pain and the responsibility for the pain. The *APA Dictionary* defines an introjection as:

1. a process in which an individual unconsciously incorporates aspects of reality external to himself or herself into the self, particularly the attitudes, values, and qualities of another person or part of another person's personality. Interjection may occur for example in the mourning process for a loved one.

2. In psychoanalytic theory, the process of internalizing the qualities of an external object into the psyche in the form of an internal object or mental representation which then has an influence on behavior. This process is posited to be a normal part of development, as when introjection of parental values and attitudes forms the superego but may also be used as a defense mechanism in situations that arouse anxiety.

According to Gestalt theory, which is known for its graphic descriptions, an introjection is when an individual psychologically swallows something whole without chewing on it. In order to remain healthy, an individual needs to psychologically chew on things, only ingesting what is nourishing and psychologically rejecting or spitting out what is not nourishing. In abusive/trauma situations, children and adolescents swallow both the pain and the responsibility for the pain as a whole introjection. Since children and adolescents need psychological nourishment (love), they have no recourse but to keep looking to the abuser(s) for their nourishment. The parasite now is in power, playing various parts of the children's or adolescents' thoughts and feelings. "I need to be very good tonight, and if I am very good, mommy will not drink. Mommy promised that if I am very good, mommy will not drink and she will not beat me. Mommy drank and beat me really hard with my baseball bat again tonight. I am so bad. I am sorry, mommy, because I am so bad. I will be better tomorrow, mommy, I promise." I know this is horrible. Yet this is what keeps me writing and hopefully keeps you reading because you and I know that you can do something to help ease this kind of incredible pain.

We need to examine one more definition that could be very important and helpful to you. The *APA Dictionary of Psychology* defines an introjective personality as, "according to some psychoanalytic theories, a line of personality development that is focused on achievement and evaluation and—if the personality fails to develop properly—may result in feelings of worthlessness, failure and psychopathological self-criticism." Once the parasite has baited or seduced the child or adolescent into absorbing the pain and the responsibility for the pain, and incorporating his or her inability to stop the pain, the child or adolescent has no recourse but to feel a sense of worthlessness and failure and to begin the psychopathological self-criticism. The parasite is now able to force the child or adolescent into the dichotomous or polarized thinking we spoke about in chapter 8. "I am all bad, and mommy is all good. I need to be perfect. I need to please people all the time. Daddy tells me I am selfish and I do not want to be selfish, so I must be selfless. I trust everyone or I trust no one. I am no damn good so it does not matter if I act that way."

I have been treating Sally for the past five years. Sally, now a 34-year-old single woman, is the youngest of three sisters. When Sally was 11, her mother died at home of a sudden massive heart attack. Sally was at home and witnessed the tragedy. After her mother's death, her father became quite despondent and was completely emotionally unavailable. Then a male teacher began to take Sally under his wing. He was kind and told her he wanted to help her with her grief. Sally, feeling totally lost and alone, took much consolation from being special to Mr. X. In time, Mr. X's special caring hugs became intense passionate kisses. Sally would freeze when this happened, but she needed his attention. One day, Mr. X took Sally to the janitor's closet. He opened his zipper and said, "Show me just how much you like me." Sally reported to me that it was as if she was there, but she was not there. "It was as if I could see myself doing this to him, but I really wasn't there." Trips to the janitor's closet continued until Sally was 14. It took her until then to have the ability to stop the insanity. Mr. X had his way with her orally, vaginally, and anally at least once a week. Sally never told anyone. I am the first and only person to know about her abuse/trauma. She came to me shortly after reading of Mr. X's death in the paper.

I have met numerous patients who have had an intense self-loathing. Sally's self-loathing was the most intense I have seen to date. Sally told me that when she read of Mr. X's death, she felt relieved and happy. In her next statement, her parasite said, "Now how sick is that?" I responded, "I do not think it is sick. I think it is most understandable and quite human." Her parasite in turn responded, "It is your job to patronize people, isn't it?" At the time I met Sally, she was grossly overweight. Her parasitic self-loathing triggered an excessive weight gain, which started around the age of 15. Her parasite told her that food was the only thing that could comfort her. There would be no more confidants, no more friends, no more teachers. The parasite also created a somewhat conscious notion that not only would food comfort her, but her obesity would protect her. "I am so fat that no one could ever want me. Besides, now I could never fit into the closet." She ate to feel comforted. This did provide her with protection but she hated herself for being obese. So, she ate to feel comforted for that self-hatred. Do you see the boundary violation? Do you see how vulnerable this 11-year-old child was? Do you hold her responsible for her abuse/trauma? Do you see the parasitic cycle of self-abuse? Do you see the parasitic absorption of the pain and the responsibility for the pain? Do you sense what Sally needs to do to heal? Most importantly, do you sense what you need to do to heal?

Sally needed to realize her innocence in this abusive/traumatic situation. Her disease was relentless in pushing the fact that she knew it was wrong and did nothing to stop the abuse/trauma. The more I would encourage her to examine the facts as she presented them to me, the more reasons the parasite would present to her in order to continue to hold her responsible. We worked at establishing the reality of what it was like for the 11-year-old.

She had just lost her mother. Her father was emotionally unavailable. She was lost and very vulnerable and easy prey for Mr. X. Eventually, Sally did concede and admit she would never hold another 11-year-old responsible for what happened to her. It appeared that the parasite finally let go of this aspect of her abuse/trauma. Her parasite was cunning, shrewd, and very powerful. It simply latched onto another aspect of her abuse/trauma. The parasite would maintain she was still responsible, not because she enjoyed the abuse/trauma, but because she enjoyed being special to Mr. X. My work with Sally reinforced the idea that in abuse/trauma situations, we need to view psychological therapy as being similar to radiation therapy and not chemotherapy. We needed to direct our energies at precisely radiating the parasite. What was happening in counseling to this point appeared to both of us that the process of our therapy was analogous to being in an amusement park and playing the whack-a-mole game. As soon as we would pound down one mole, another would surface, and on and on. Only we were not at an amusement park and it was not fun. Sally was in tremendous pain and she was not getting better. Sally needed to recognize what was parasitic and what was Sally. As previously indicated, Sally and you need to listen closely to the chatter in your head. You and Sally need to identify when the parasite is bombarding you with the illogical and irrational statements. You and Sally need to counter the illogical and irrational statements with logic and reason. Perhaps it sounds too simple. It is not as simple as it seems. Remember the five P's. This process demands much patience and persistence. You must keep radiating the parasite until it begins to shrink. Once you begin to perceive that the parasite is shrinking, the hope of healing begins to genuinely root inside of you.

A turning point in Sally's counseling was when she began to put boundaries on her sense of responsibility. Sally was able to make an incredible shift in her thinking. She began to embrace that she could be responsible *to* her pain without being responsible *for* it. This shift in the sense of responsibility afforded Sally enough energy to begin promoting her healing rather than continuing with her cycle of self-abuse. While it was very difficult for her to accept the disease model, she came to perceive the parasite as her enemy instead of the various psychological parts of her and, in particular, the 11-year-old. Cautiously, she began to actually communicate with the various parts of her ego through visual imagery. This communication enabled Sally to create an agreement with all the parts of her to use her anger to attack the parasite rather than herself. She had held her 11-year-old part and her insatiable eating part responsible for her pain and suffering. She began to eventually perceive that it was the parasite that was her enemy and not the parts of her ego. She actually embraced the dynamics of how the parasite, using the self-abusive cycle to create her intense self-loathing, would have eventually consumed her. Her anger over the abuse became her best ally in attacking the parasite. The anger she felt provided her with the necessary psychological energy to begin reestablishing the boundary within herself. Eventually, Sally took that subtle but powerful shift and began establishing a boundary on her sense of responsibility. She also began putting boundaries on her eating behaviors. In a year and a half, she lost an incredible amount of weight. You might ask, "How much weight?" I do not know. As much as I know about Sally and as much as she has shared with me, she will not reveal how much weight she has lost. When I asked, she smiled and said, "This is where I have established a healthy boundary, Doc. Do not violate it."

Sally's situation exemplifies the need for the establishment or reestablishment of healthy boundaries. The boundary of being responsible to her pain and not for it allowed her to begin to trust herself. She like so many others of my patients learned a new word in therapy. This new word is no. No, I do not have to please everyone all the time. I can choose when I want to do things that are pleasing to others. No, I do not have to be perfect. When I do my best, I can feel good about doing my best even when I do not achieve all that I set out to achieve. No, I do not have to be a doormat. No, I do not have to compensate for being inferior because I am not inferior. Sally, using baby steps in a slow but steady pace, began to see the gray in the world. More times than not, the gray appeared frightening to Sally, but in Sally's own words, "not nearly as frightening as the black and white world her parasite created for her." Sally learned that selfish and selfless are polarities on a continuum. In order to avoid being selfish, an attribute she despised, the parasite conned her into being selfless. Her selflessness became a complete hell for her, a hell she had great difficulty escaping. Whenever she said no to a person's request, the parasite collapsed sadness into guilt. The parasite played her into believing that if she felt guilty, she must be doing something wrong. In response to this belief, she quickly learned to never say no to anyone's request. Yet, she found herself feeling angry and resentful of always doing things for others. You know, I am not asking you to become selfish. I personally dislike selfish people. I will go out of my way to help people. When I choose to do something, it becomes empowering. When I have to, or I should, or I must, the task becomes a burden. This is when we begin to feel anger, frustration, and resentment. *Webster's Dictionary* defines selfless as "having little concern for oneself and one's interest." It also defined selfish as "caring only or

chiefly for oneself; concern with one's own interest regardless of others."
It is clear that both polarities are unhealthy. Most developmental psychologists agree that balance is crucial to healthy functioning. Establishing or
reestablishing pliable and intact boundaries is the key to balance. Pliable
is an important term in the description of healthy boundaries. Pliability is
really flexibility, meaning that in some situations where you really trust
the person, you can drop your guard. In other situations where trust is an
unknown, you are able to keep your guard up. The term pliability allows
you to move away from the polarities of complete trust, and no trust at all.
Keep in mind that an individual in your life needs to earn your trust. Never
give trust to someone just because of status, credentials, or position. You
have both the need and the right to ensure, as best as one can, that you have
a sense of safety and security in the relationship. With these thoughts in
mind, you can begin to develop healthy pliable boundaries.

# TEN

## Fragmented, Not Damaged

One of the most common self-descriptive words used by individuals who have suffered the torment of childhood abuse/trauma is the word *damaged*. To date, every patient I have treated with a history of abuse/trauma has used this word to describe themselves. Bill Zeller in his suicide note used the word damaged twice to describe himself. You are probably saying to yourself, "But this is exactly how I feel, and you cannot tell me how to feel." I know this is how you feel, and you are most correct in that I cannot tell you how to feel. In chapter 5, we discussed the notion that feelings certainly are real to the individual and represent the person's internal reality. While your feelings represent your internal reality, your feelings do not necessarily represent the external reality and are not always grounded in objective reality. Throughout a significant portion of this text, I have repeatedly stated that you are not damaged. Perhaps, as you kept hearing me say that you are not damaged, you became upset with me just as you may have been upset with me in my use of the word victim. Know that I am not telling you how to feel, nor am I invalidating your feelings, nor am I attempting to minimize your feelings. I am simply attempting to point out an objective reality. Nowhere in psychology is the word damaged used to describe a person. Nowhere in the *Diagnostic and Statistical Manual IV TR,* which contains all the psychological diagnoses, does the word damaged appear to describe an individual, or the individual's symptomatology. Well, if you are not damaged or worse yet, broken, what is making you feel like you are damaged or broken? It is the parasite powerfully telling you that you are damaged or broken in order to keep you feeling helpless and hopeless and thus allowing the parasite to maintain its infectious grip on your ego. Your abuse/trauma caused ego fragmentation, and ego fragmentation is completely different from being damaged or broken.

You have already read several references to the Gestalt parts model. This school of psychology theorizes that the ego is comprised of many parts, and healthy human functioning requires a fair degree of integration of these various parts of the ego (Murdock, 2009). Your abuse/trauma and the introjection of the contaminants have resulted in the various parts of your ego isolating, rather than integrating. This isolation of the parts of your ego has resulted in your ego fragmentation, not ego damage, nor ego brokenness. Abuse/trauma is analogous to a person experiencing a sudden explosion. Imagine, if you will, you are in your apartment. It is very late and you are just beginning to unwind from a very hectic day. All of a sudden with no warning, you hear a loud noise and your apartment begins to shake. You are terrified. You get out of bed to discover what happened. You attempt to turn the lights on, but there is no electricity. You stumble around to find a flashlight and search your apartment to ascertain what has happened. You cannot locate the source of the noise or what caused your apartment to actually shake. You finally go to bed but cannot sleep. It is now morning, and you proceed suspiciously to locate the culprit responsible for the loud noise and the trembling of your apartment and to make sure everything is okay. You cannot locate the cause of the noise or the rumbling, but you are still apprehensive that something may be wrong. This feeling can stay with you for days or weeks. Now, if you would, think back to a younger you. The abuse/trauma, the explosion, came out of nowhere, without any warning. The various parts of your ego went on high alert to ascertain what happened, and what injury, if any, resulted from this explosion. The abuse/trauma caused a total collapse of your equilibrium. The parasite appeared on the scene immediately after the explosion. Because all the parts of you were on high alert, which is Selye's (1936) alarm stage, none of the parts of your ego recognized the parasite as an intruder. Keep in mind that the parasite was contained in, and disguised as, contaminated love. There was no way any part or parts of you could have known about the contamination and the parasite. Your ego defenses were down as the ego was open to receive nourishing love. The various parts of you were in a trusting mode expecting to receive nourishment (love), which is essential to the ego's health. The parasite began to take charge, and as it took charge of the crisis, it initiated the blaming of one part or another for the explosion. The blaming, the making sense of no sense, began to afford the ego with a false sense of equilibrium. With the blaming of the part or parts of you, all parts of you remained isolated from one another.

Thus, your ego became fragmented, and because of the parasite's power and control, it has remained fragmented, not damaged, and not broken as you have felt.

Let me emphasize this important point once more. The parasite initially manipulated numerous parts of the ego into believing that a part or parts of the self were responsible for the abuse/trauma. An ongoing war connived by the parasite had been declared within your ego. There have been many casualties. It only takes one episode of the abuse/trauma for the contaminants to be ingested. The one episode is sufficient for the parasite, with a mind of its own, to create ego fragmentation amidst the chaos of abuse/trauma. Unfortunately, we know that abuse/trauma is rarely, if ever, a one-time event. The more the child or adolescent experiences abuse/trauma, the stronger the parasite becomes. The stronger the parasite becomes, the more it manipulates the parts of the ego to maintain ego fragmentation, until the parasite destroys trust within and among the parts of the ego. With the parts of the ego at war with itself, and the resulting mistrust of the self, the parasite is free to attempt an invasion of the psyche (or the soul) of the individual. The psyche contains the essence of the individual. If the parasite is able to infect the psyche, the parasite can and will eventually destroy the person either physically or psychospiritually. In the case of Bill Zeller, the parasite was able to breach the psyche resulting in his completed suicide. The more the parasite tells you that you are damaged, the more this concept becomes rooted into your ego. The result is less self-worth, less self-regard, and less self-respect. This diminished self-worth, regard, and respect only serves to intensify the war among the parts of the self.

Accepting and believing that your ego is fragmented but not damaged or broken is yet another crucial aspect of healing. You might be asking, "Is there really a difference between fragmented and damaged?" There definitely is a difference, and, yes, I am going to provide you with another definition. *Webster's Dictionary* defines damaged as "injury or harm that reduces value or usefulness." The parasite has been taunting you with the word damaged for years. I know the patients that I have worked with in counseling felt reduced in value. The parasite has used this tactic over and over in their minds and in your mind. The parasite has over time truly convinced them and you that you are less than other people. With the parasite playing the various parts of your ego against you, you have absorbed the guilt and the responsibility for your abuse/trauma. The absorption of the guilt and responsibility has resulted in your incredible sense of shame and self-doubt. You have developed your perfectionism and people-pleasing characteristics in order to compensate for your sense of being damaged and all the resulting negativity that accompanies being damaged.

It is perhaps important to reexamine some of the child developmental theory of Jean Piaget contained in chapter 4. Piaget (1954) postulated that the child adapts to his or her world through the processes of assimilation and accommodation. Through the process of assimilation, the child takes information from the outside environment and begins to incorporate this information into his or her thinking even though this new information may be contrary to the child's senses. An example of this would be, the child being told how incredibly bad and evil he or she is, as opposed to the child's own sense of being good. The child will assimilate this information from the environment in order to accommodate this new information. Therefore, the child may sense that he or she is good but having been told that he or she is bad, the child adapts to this information, assimilates the new data, and makes the necessary accommodations for the new information of being bad and evil. A very simple example for this complex theory is as follows. You take your son or daughter who is three years old and who has never seen farm animals to a petting zoo. The first animals you encounter are cows and you exclaim, "Look, these animals are cows. They go moo." The child mimics this and says, "Cows go moo." The child has assimilated the information about cows. Cows are four-legged large animals that moo. His senses will tell him that any four-legged, large animal will be a cow. Next, you visit the horses, and the child immediately exclaims, "Cows, they go moo." And of course you say, "No, these are horses." The child needs to accommodate this information regardless of what his senses tell him. An easy way to appreciate accommodation is to think of accommodation as differentiating one thing from another. The parasite manipulated you into assimilating that you were damaged, and you accommodated this sense of being damaged. In order to compensate for being damaged, you adapted to this faulty information by developing your perfectionism and people-pleasing characteristics. Through this parasitic manipulation, you became absorbed in a vicious cycle of self-defeat. Since you can never be perfect or please people perfectly, the parasitic notion of being damaged was continually being reinforced.

This, believe it or not, is actually a quite normal adaptation to an abnormal and completely dysfunctional situation. What I am saying is that considering the abuse/trauma experiences you endured, your ego responded in a reasonable manner to adapt to an insane environment. The adaptive response and the assimilation and accommodation to the abuse/trauma, while dysfunctional, are most understandable and quite ingenious. Having

been baited by the parasite to adapt in this fashion, the child's or adolescent's ego simply could not comprehend the impossibility of this attempted adaptation. In essence, while the adaptation was dysfunctional
and served to create more and more pain for you, it was simultaneously
quite functional on some level.

"So if I am not damaged, what am I?" You are fragmented, or more
accurately stated, your ego is fragmented. Something tells me you might
be thinking, "Here he goes with his word games again." No, that is truly
not what I am doing. Remember, it is your parasite that has played word
games in order to create a vicious cycle of abuse and self-abuse. Reexamine Figure 7.1 on page 111. If you are going to work at radiating the parasite and work at shrinking it, you need to be equipped with more accurate
data in order to counter the parasitic word games. *Fragmented* is very different from *damaged*. *Webster's Dictionary* in defining fragmented uses
terms that include, "an isolated part, or disunity." Clearly, you can see the
definite difference in the terms *damaged* and *fragmented*.

Abuse/trauma has created a fragmentation or a disenfranchising of the
parts of your ego. Some of the parts of your ego, manipulated by the parasite, actually blame some other parts of you for the abuse/trauma. As a
result of the blaming, the parasite has baited many of the parts of you to
attempt to remove, exclude, or contain the parts of yourself responsible for
the pain. When you stop and truly ponder this effort, this does make perfect sense. Remember the biblical concept that if the eye is an occasion of
sin, then you must pluck it out. If you had a sudden attack of appendicitis,
the doctors would tell you that it is best to remove the appendix. It is the
source of your pain and it can cause more pain and perhaps even death. It
is only logical then that if a part of me is responsible for all my pain, why
not simply get rid of it? Then I will not be bad and I will not be in pain.
This sounds logical to a child or adolescent, perhaps even to an adult, who
does not fully comprehend the irrationality and impossibility of this kind
of psychic surgery. You can surgically remove your appendix. You cannot
surgically remove any part or parts of your ego because all the parts are
vital to your emotional health and stability.

Perhaps, by now, as you are reading this chapter, you might feel as if
you have more questions than answers. You may be thinking to yourself,
"I have had this feeling of being damaged for so long that it feels as if
it is a part of me. I do not know if I can let go of this horrible feeling. I
am not even sure that there really is a difference between feeling damaged and feeling fragmented." Let me assure you again that there really
is a difference between damaged and fragmented. Go back and read the

definitions. Stop using the word damaged in reference to yourself and replace it with the word fragmented. This will not miraculously replace the feeling of being damaged, but it is a start. You will need to communicate with the various parts of your ego. This communication can readily be accomplished through the use of various counseling techniques. Before providing you with some examples of these techniques, it is important to present you with some information regarding how we learn. Psychology informs us that there are three channels available and utilized in our learning process. There is the auditory channel where we learn by hearing. Sometimes we can actually produce audiotapes of conversations or lectures, and so forth, in our heads. There is the kinesthetic channel, which involves more tactile aspects of learning. If you are into baking or making pasta dough, you learn by the feel of the texture of the batter or the dough. There is also the visual channel wherein learning occurs by you making pictures in your mind of what needs to be learned. All three channels are available to us and we use all three. However, each of us has a favorite channel, and in times of distress we will utilize that favorite channel. Since we have not had the opportunity to meet, there is no way I can tell what your favorite channel is. But if you think long and hard, and listen to the verbs you use, you will be able to ascertain your favorite learning channel. Verbs such as hear, listen, talk, and so forth are auditory verbs. Verbs such as grasp, hold, touch, and the like are kinesthetic verbs, while verbs such as look, see, pictures, and so on are visual verbs. Some of my patients have used the technique of journaling to communicate with the various parts of their ego. The technique of journaling is more of the kinesthetic technique. Other patients who are visual learners have used the technique of visual imagery to communicate with their parts. You will know what techniques will be helpful for you to accomplish this communication with the parts of your ego. Be aware of the fact that some of the parts of your ego have been quite isolated for a considerable period of time. You will need to develop a sense of trust with the parts of you, and the parts of you will also need to develop a sense of trust in you. It may be necessary for you to seek forgiveness from the isolated parts and to give forgiveness to these isolated parts of you.

After assimilating and accommodating the word fragmented into both your mind and heart, you will begin to experience some genuine shifts in your thoughts and feelings. The sense of tremendous shame and doubt that you have carried will actually begin to diminish. As this shame and doubt diminishes, there will be a shift in your thinking regarding your perception of your responsibility for the abuse/trauma. You will be afforded the energy to make the split in your responsibility. You will assume responsibility to heal your pain rather than holding yourself responsible for your pain. You then will be able to feel the necessity and logic of splitting the emotions of guilt and sadness. This will allow you to appropriately grieve the loss of your childhood or adolescence and/or a parent or parents. All of these things will give you the energy and the strength and the courage to continuously radiate the parasite until the parasite eventually loses its grip on the part or parts of you. This perhaps may not be the exact road map you utilize in the journey of healing. If need be, use this only as a template to develop your own road map. I encourage you to develop your own road map based on your needs and your situation. You will feel discouraged from time to time. That is normal and natural. Do not allow yourself to get stuck in this discouragement. The parasite will use that as energy. Keep all the energy you have and use it for your healing and do not allow the parasite to use it for your destruction.

Several of my patients, after working on the first two stages of healing, moved directly to this fragmented, not damaged, stage of healing. They were able to find great consolation in the reality that they were not damaged but rather simply fragmented. One patient put it eloquently, "It was as if a huge boulder that I had been carrying for so long was lifted off my shoulders. I felt energized and alive for the first time in a very long time." It is my wish that you will stop using the term damaged and use in its place the term fragmented. It is my hope and prayer that you will feel the burden that you have been carrying lifted off your shoulders and that you will feel energized and alive.

# ELEVEN

## The Story of the Journey of Your Healing

Author's note: This chapter is purposefully left blank for you to write your story.

Will you work at writing the story of your journey toward healing?

Will you perceive the goodness that exists in you?

Will you come to know that your abuse/trauma is only a part of you, not all of you?

Will you commit to living in the moment and live that moment as a pathway to your future?

Will you commit to forgiving yourself and loving yourself?

Will you come to embrace the strength, courage, and resilience that has brought you this far?

Will you work at recognizing and radiating the parasite?

Will you take your Spirit with you on this journey?

# A Concluding Note

Life is a journey, not a destination.

*—Ralph Waldo Emerson*

The words of Mr. Emerson are very powerful and very fitting. I would ask you to do two things. One is to change the word *life* and replace it with the word *healing*. Two is to keep this quote in the forefront of your mind each waking moment of your life. In the Introduction, I stated that this text was being written to provide you with hope in your struggle with abuse/trauma and to provide you with a pathway for you to heal the incredible pain you experienced. My prayer is that I accomplished this goal. I also stated in the Introduction that another aspiration for this text was to provide my patients, whose stories you have read, with some additional meaning for their suffering. They tell me that this aspiration has been met. I know I have placed before you many very difficult tasks. Embrace the fact that while these tasks may be very difficult, none of them are impossible. I know that inside of you lie the strength, resilience, and courage necessary for your healing. I ask you to trust in yourself that these wonderful healing qualities are truly there. "Seek and you will find" (Luke 11:9).

We live in an incredibly fast-paced world. We can see live videos of situations occurring across the globe. You can shop for an item online at three o'clock in the morning and have it in your possession within a day. The media is overflowing with advertisements of instant relief from any type of pain. Even the advertisements for antidepressants make it appear that the depressed person recovers instantly. We have come to expect that everything in our lives should be instant. To speak of patience is almost countercultural. However, the healing process of emotional, physical, and spiritual issues is never instantaneous. The birthing process requires nine months. A woman who is six months pregnant may become tired of being pregnant and want to give birth today. No matter what the expecting mother wants, the fetus will not be born one minute before its time, so the mother needs to be patient. You will need to be patient with your healing process and with yourself. I know that for someone who is in pain a minute or even the second is too long. Unfortunately, patience is an essential element in order to effect true healing.

In addition to patience, you will need to examine the process of healing. In our Western culture, we have become event-oriented. We mark births, deaths, anniversaries, and holidays as discrete events. Rarely, if ever, do we examine the process that often leads to these events? In regard to healing, you need to appreciate the process. I tell my students repeatedly that counseling is a process not an event. Each session is analogous to an individual link in a chain, one building on the other to form the chain. If we go back to the pregnancy analogy, it becomes clear that pregnancy is a process not an event. Certainly, it begins with conception, which might appear to be an event. However, if we were to examine this closely, conception typically includes the process of people falling in love, learning to trust one another, desiring intimacy, and so on. I am sure you get the point. You have engaged in the process of healing. This process requires patience and necessitates that you fully engage in the process. If you were ever on vacation or a trip with young children, you know that 10 minutes away from home they start the "Are we there yet?" questions. Somehow that anticipation never really leaves us, even as adults. You will need to think about your healing in terms of one day at a time, one moment at a time. You and I both know you want to be healed and you wanted to be healed yesterday. Regrettably, this is impossible. Each day you awaken and choose to work at your healing, you are one step closer to your goal. You are one step closer to subduing the parasite. There will be days you feel you took one step forward and three steps backward. You will inevitably at times feel defeated. Validate this feeling, but work at not allowing the parasite to overwhelm you with this feeling. Remember, being on the journey itself, choosing life-giving behaviors over self-defeating behaviors is a critical aspect to your healing. When you fall, simply get up. Brush yourself off, work at forgiving yourself for being human, and continue on your journey. Never lose sight of your goal.

As humans we have shortcomings, imperfections, and frailties. Healing is a lifelong process, and healing does not mean you will arrive at some level of perfection. Always know that perfection is a total impossibility. Healing involves coming to terms with being human and accepting our shortcomings. Healing involves us coming to terms with simply doing our best and thus leaving the rest to the Spirit.

I have said many times in this text that some of the thoughts and concepts might seem to be redundant. I also explained that the redundancy was purposeful. Therapy or counseling is a redundant process. It must be redundant at times in order to allow for the full unlearning of faulty beliefs and the relearning of healthier, more adaptive beliefs. Competent therapists rarely tell their clients or patients anything that the client or patient, at some level, does not already know. The therapist's job, then, is to place before the client what the client already knows. But it is presented in a manner that affords the client the opportunity to see more clearly, or hear differently, or grasp onto it in a more useful way. When you lose sight, or do not hear as well, or lose your grasp on the issue, it is often necessary to go over old material. This is normal and truly a part of the process.

You have already heard me say several times how much I have learned from my patients. I hope to learn from you as well. In order to do that, I am creating a website as this manuscript goes to print. I encourage you to ask questions, make recommendations where you feel the text could have been more helpful, or explain what was helpful to you. I ask you to be as specific as possible. If that is not something you feel comfortable doing, I would ask you to go on the Amazon, Barnes & Noble, Books A Million, or any other book sites and write a review of your thoughts about this book, both positive and negative. As a professor, my students evaluate my teaching each semester. I always ask that they be precise. Just saying the course was great, while flattering, does not really help me understand what made it great. On the other hand, just telling me the course sucked does not help me rectify the issues. If we are to refine a methodology to assist survivors, we need to hear from the experts—you. I ask you to express your thoughts so we can accomplish this goal.

This text was not intended to be digested in one reading or in one week. If after reading it you found some concepts particularly useful, go back and reread those sections. If you find yourself losing sight, or sound, or grip on something you want to work on for your journey, go over and over those pages until the concept sinks into your belief system. Normalize your discouragement and validate these feelings. You can then focus your energy on the healing process and subduing the parasite. Keep your focus on winning the war, not every battle. One concept in the process of healing that I have not strongly addressed is courage. You will need much courage in your war with the parasite. I know you have that courage. Again, look inside and ask all the parts of you to muster the necessary courage to fight this good fight. Make sure you involve your Spirit in this good fight. You will be amazed at how important and helpful this will be. Remember to embrace your fear. Your fear does not make you a coward; it just wants you to survive and that is a very healthy issue. Heroes are not individuals who feel no fear. They are individuals who do what is necessary in spite of their fear. It takes courage to dream your dreams and it will take courage to actualize your dreams. Start by having the courage to dream. The more you dream, the stronger the dream will become and the more courage you will have. The more courageous you become, the easier it will be to make your dreams realities. I will leave you with a poem written by Leslie Nielson titled "Believe in All That You Are."

Shalom


### Believe in All That You Are*

As the dawn of each morning

peers into your life,

there lies a path to follow.

Delicate whispers can be heard

if you listen to the sound of your heart

and the voice that speaks within you.


If you listen closely to your soul,

you will become aware of your dreams

that are yet to unfold.

You will discover that there lies within you

a voice of confidence and strength

---

*The poem "Believe in All That You Are" by Leslie Nielson is from *Keep Believing in Yourself and Your Special Dreams*. Copyright (c) 2002 by Blue Mountain Arts, Inc. Reprinted by permission. All Rights Reserved.

that will prompt you to seek a journey

and live a dream.


Within the depths of your mind,

the purpose and direction of your life

can be determined by listening intently

to the knowledge that you already possess.

Your heart, mind, and soul

are the foundation

of your success and happiness.


In the still of each passing moment,

may you come to understand that

you are capable of reaching a higher destiny.

When you come to believe in all that you are

and all that you can become,

there will be no cause for doubt.

Believe in your heart, for it offers hope.

Believe in your mind, for it offers direction.

Believe in your soul, for it offers strength.

But above all else . . . believe in yourself.

*—Leslie Nielson*

# An Invitation to Clinicians...

In this text, I have proposed a model to assist survivors of abuse/trauma. Some of the aspects proposed such as utilizing the disease model, the metaphor of the parasite, and even the use of spirituality can be viewed by many clinicians as outside the box. If you are treating those survivors of abuse/trauma, you know the impact abuse/trauma has on the individual. In order to address these complexities, I have purposely gone outside the box. The proposed methodology has been presented at state, regional, national, and international conferences and has been well received by our colleagues. This methodology was never intended to be the last word on treating adult survivors. It is, however, intended to create much dialogue for those of us who are willing to work with the atrocities committed against our clients by people who were suppose to love and protect them.

In my work over the last 20 years, I have used this model successfully. However, I am acutely aware of the limited number of patients I have treated as opposed to all the individuals out there who have suffered childhood and adult abuse/trauma. In addition, there is always the aspect of experimenter bias. As I informed the survivor readers, I am creating a website to allow for feedback from them and from you, the clinician, regarding the efficacy of the proposed model. My ultimate goal is to collect enough data to ascertain whether this model could qualify as an empirically validated treatment protocol. In order to do this, we need to work together. If you are willing to join me in this endeavor, we will need to establish baseline data and instrumentation necessary to document whether or not this proposed model can be used in a variety of settings and with a variety of individuals. As a clinician, I know what you don't need is more work. However, working together, I am confident we can obtain data that neither taxes the client nor the clinician. If you are not willing to participate in this endeavor, it would be very important for me to know the reasons you choose not to participate. The reason may be the model itself, the metaphor of the parasite, the use of spirituality, lack of time, or some other issue. I believe it is critically important that I ascertain this information, which may lead to critical revisions to assist our clients. If you choose not to use the website, I would again encourage you to write a review on Amazon, Barnes & Nobles or any other book review site and in clude specific positive and negative comments. I look forward to working with you.

# Bibliography

Aber, J., & Allen, J. (1987). Effects of maltreatment on young children's socio-emotional development: An attached theory perspective. *Developmental Psychology, 23,* 406–414.

Ainsworth, M. (1978). *Patterns of attachment: A psychological study of the strange situation.* Hillsdale, NJ: Lawrence Erlbaum Associates.

Berne, E. (1961). *Transactional analysis in psychotherapy.* New York: Grove Press.

Berne, E. (1964). *Games people play.* New York: Grove Press.

Bohart, A., & Todd, J. (1988). *Foundations of clinical and counseling psychology.* New York: Harper & Row.

Boriosi, G. D. (2002). *Understanding yourself: It's so darn easy.* Danbury, CT: Rutledge Books.

Bowlby, J. (1988). *A secure base: Parent–child attachment and healthy human development.* New York: Basic Books.

Coker, L. S. (1990). A therapeutic recovery model for the female adult incest survivor. *Issues in Mental Health: Nursing, 11,* 109–123.

Enright, R. D., & Fitzgibbons, R. P. (2000). *Helping clients forgive: An empirical guide for resolving anger and restoring hope.* Washington, DC: American Psychological Association.

Erikson, E. (1963). *Childhood and society.* New York: Norton.

Fowler, J. (1981). *Stages of faith: The psychology of human development and the quest for meaning.* San Francisco, CA: Harper & Row.

Frankie Perez's Mindgym (2010). *Four keys to self-acceptance.* Retrieved from http://www.facebook.com/topic.php?uid = 362541047781&topic = 12695.

Freud, S. (1955). Lines of advance in psychoanalytic theory. In J. Strachey (Ed.), *The standard edition of the complete psychological works of Sigmund Freud* (Vol. 17). London: Hogarth Press. (Original work published 1918).

Glasser, W. (2010). *Thinkexist.com quotations online.* Retrieved from www. quotesdaddy.com/authors/w/William_glasser_2.html.

Groze, V., & Rosenthal, J. (1993). Attachment theory and the adoption of children with special needs. *Social Work Research and Abstracts, 29,* 5–12.

Inhelder, B., & Piaget, J. (1964). *The early growth of logic in the child, classification and seriation.* New York: Harper & Row.

Kohlberg, L. (1984). *The psychology of moral development: The nature and validity of moral stages.* San Francisco: Harper and Row.

Kübler-Ross, Elisabeth (1969). *On death and dying* (1st ed.). New York: Touchstone.

Kushner, H. (1981). *When bad things happen to good people.* New York: Random House.

Lau, E., & Donnan, S. (1987). Maternal and child factors for reported child abuse among Chinese in Hong Kong. *Social Science and Medicine, 24,* 449–452.

Lemoncelli, J. (2008). *A mind of its own: Healing the mind and heart of the parasite of childhood abuse.* Eynon, PA: Avventura Press.

Lemoncelli, J., & Carey, A. (1996). The psychospiritual dynamics of adult survivors. *Counseling and Values, 4 (3),* 53–64. (Reprinted by permission of ACA.)

Lynch, M., & Cicchetti, D. (1992). Maltreated children's reports of relatedness to their teachers. *New Directions for Child Development, 57,* 81–107.

Magid, K., & McKelvey, C. (1989). *High risk: Children without a conscience.* New York: Bantam.

Mahler, M. (1968). *On human symbiosis and vicissitudes of individuals: Vol. I. Infantile psychosis.* New York: International Press.

Mahler, M., Pine, F., & Bergman, A. (1975). *The psychological birth of the human infant.* New York: Basic Books.

Maslow, A. (1954). *Motivation and personality.* New York: Harper & Row.

Monat, A., & Lazarus, R. (1977). *Stress and coping: An anthology.* New York: Columbia University Press.

Murdock, N. (2009). *Theories of counseling and psychotherapy: A case approach* (2nd ed.). Upper Saddle River, NJ: Pearson.

Neilson, Leslie (2002). *Believe in all that you are: Keep believing in yourself and your special dream.* Boulder, CO: Blue Mountain Arts. (Reprinted by permission.)

Perls, Fritz (1969). *In and out the garbage pail.* Chicago: Gestalt Journal Press.

Piaget, J. (1954). *The construction of reality in the child.* New York: Basic Books.

Salmon, J. (2008, June 24). Most Americans believe in a higher power, poll finds. *Washington Post,* A02. Retrieved from http://washingtonpost.com

Schweitzer, R., & Lawton, P. (1989). Drug abusers' perceptions of their parents. *British Journal of Addiction, 84,* 309–314.

Seyle, H. (1936). A syndrome produced by diverse nocuous agents. *Journal of Neuropsychiatry and Clinical Neurosciences,* 32–34.

Selye, H. (1956). *The stress of life.* New York: McGraw-Hill.

Selye, H. (1967). *Stress: Sources, management, and prevention.* New York: Liveright Publishing Company.

Selye, H. (1974). *Stress without distress.* New York: J. B. Lippincott.

Sullivan, H. (1972). *Personal psychopathology.* New York: Norton.

VandenBos, Gary (Ed. in Chief). (2007). *APA Dictionary of Psychology* (1st ed.). Washington, DC: American Psychological Association.

*Webster's Universal College Dictionary.* (2004). New York: Gramercy.

Whitfield, C. (1989). *Healing the child within: Discovery and recovery for adult children of dysfunctional families.* Deerfield Beach, FL: Health Communications.

Zeller, Bill (2011, January). Princeton grad student and brilliant programmer, dies in apparent suicide. *Huffpost College.* Retrieved from http://www.huffing tonpost.com.

# Index

## About the Author

**John J. Lemoncelli, EdD,** is a tenured Professor in the Graduate Psychology and Counseling Department of Marywood University, Scranton, Pennsylvania. He is also the Assistant Chair for the Counseling Program. He maintained a part-time private practice for nearly 30 years where he specialized in the treatment of adult survivors of abuse and clergy. He has written articles and has given numerous presentations on the topics of ethics, spirituality and psychotherapy, and treating adult survivors of abuse. He is licensed by the Commonwealth of Pennsylvania as a Psychologist and is a Licensed Professional Counselor.